Icebound IN THE SiBERIAN ARCTIC

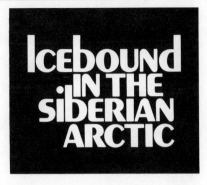

Icebound IN THE SiBERIAN ARCTIC

The story of
the last cruise
of the fur schooner
Nanuk and the
international search for
famous arctic pilot
Carl Ben Eielson

ROBERT j. GLEASON

ALASKA NORTHWEST PUBLISHING COMPANY
Anchorage, Alaska

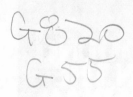

Library of Congress cataloging in publication data:
Gleason, Robert J   1906-
   Icebound in the Siberian Arctic.
   Bibliography: p.
   1. Arctic regions.   2. Nanuk (Ship)
3. Eielson, Carl Benjamin, 1897-1929.   I. Title.
G820.G55   919.8   [B]   77-1320
ISBN 0-88240-067-3

PHOTOS AND NEWS CLIPPINGS—All photos and news clippings in this book are from the author's collection. Almost all of the photos were taken by the author; a few are from collections given to him later by his companions, Chuck Huntley and Jim Hutchinson. News clippings are from a scrapbook kept by the author's family, who followed his progress in the Seattle newspapers. Credit to the source is given with the news clippings and photos by others; photos not so marked are the original work of the author.

Design by Hilber Nelson
Cover design by Roselyn Pape
CartoGraphics by Jon. Hersh
Alaska Northwest Publishing Company
Box 4-EEE, Anchorage, Alaska 99509
Printed in U.S.A.

To Joe Crosson

CONTENTS

THE ARCTIC COAST of EASTERN SIBERIA

CHAPTER 1

THIS BOOK CONCERNS A STRETCH OF THE
Siberian Arctic coast little known to Americans. It is not a story of
powerful steel ships, icebreakers, big multi-engined airplanes,
helicopters, world weather forecasting, fully-instrumented and
radio-equipped aircraft. It is not about an Arctic Expedition, nor
an adventurer deliberately seeking a record or publicity for his
self-imposed hardships. It is the story of a small, old, Pacific coast
lumber schooner's fight to traverse that coast in the summer of

1929, her forced wintering at North Cape, Siberia, and the attempts of an infant aviation industry to come to her aid. It tells how a small band of men fought the Arctic with a wooden ship and small single-engined airplanes after being trapped on a somewhat hazardous commercial venture into Arctic Siberia.

The coast involved is little known to Russians as well as to Americans, for it is the Arctic coast of the most remote part of Siberia, that from Bering Strait to the Kolyma River. There is undoubtedly still little travel to this area other than by the military people who man the radar stations and air bases which have almost certainly been built there in recent years.

This coast is unique also in that a stretch of it was the very last to be explored in the attempt to prove positively that Asia and North America were not joined together somewhere in the Arctic.

Czar Peter the Great in 1725 had commissioned Vitus Bering to build two boats in Kamchatka and sail north along the eastern shore of Siberia to determine "where it joins with America." (Bering was a Dane who had spent 20 years with the Russian navy.) After two years of struggle, first across Siberia to reach Okhotsk, and there to build two small vessels, the Russians came around the Kamchatka Peninsula and up the coast. In August, 1728, the *Saint Gabriel* stood abreast of East Cape (now *Mys Dezhneva*), and they "saw the land falling away sharply to the west," proving that Asia was not there connected to America. As they started back to the south, they sighted and named the two Diomede Islands, but poor weather denied them the sight of Cape Prince of Wales and the York Mountains only some 50 miles away on the North American side of the strait now named for Bering.

Exactly 50 years later Captain James Cook, on his third and last great voyage of exploration, came looking again from the Asian side for the long-sought passage from Europe to the Pacific—called variously the northwest passage or northeast passage, depending on the sailing direction. Sailing through the Aleutian Island's Unimak Pass into the Bering Sea, Cook explored Bristol Bay and the western coast of Alaska, including the Seward Peninsula. He crossed to the bay in Siberia he named Saint Lawrence, and then went on northward through Bering's Strait. Cook found the Arctic Ocean remarkably free of ice and was able to sail up the Alaskan coast past Point Hope and Cape Lisburne without difficulty. He was finally stopped by impenetrable pack ice at Icy Cape, which he named. He back-tracked to

Cape Lisburne and then followed the southern edge of the ice pack west to find Bering's "land falling sharply away to the west." As he neared the Siberian coast, Cook reported:

"In the morning of the 29th [August, 1788], we saw the main ice to the northward, and not long after, land bearing southwest by west. Presently after this, more land showed itself, bearing west. It showed itself in two hills like islands, but afterward the whole appeared connected. As we approached the land, the depth of water decreased very fast; so that at noon, when we tacked, we had only eight fathoms; being three miles from the coast, which extended from south, 30° east, to north, 60° west. This last extreme terminated in a bluff point, being one of the hills above mentioned. The weather at this time was very hazy, with drizzling rain; but soon after, it cleared; especially to the southward, westward, and northward. This enabled us to have a pretty good view of the coast; which, in every respect, is like the opposite one of America; that is, low land next the sea, with elevated land farther back. It was perfectly destitute of wood, and even snow; but was, probably, covered with a mossy substance, that gave it a brownish cast. In the low ground lying between the high land and the sea was a lake, extending to the southeast farther than we could see. As we stood off, the westernmost of the two hills before mentioned came open off the bluff point, in the direction of north-west. It had the appearance of being an island; but it might be joined to the other by low land, though we did not see it. And if so, there is a two-fold point, with a bay between them. This point, which is steep and rocky, was named Cape North. Its situation is nearly in the latitude of 68° 56', and in the longitude of 180° 51'. The coast beyond it must take a very western direction; for we could see no land to the northward of it, though the horizon was there pretty clear. Being desirous of seeing more of the coast to the westward, we tacked again, at two o'clock in the afternoon, thinking we could weather Cape North. But finding we could not, the wind freshening, a thick fog coming on, with much snow, and being fearful of the ice coming down upon us, I gave up the design I had formed of plying to the westward, and stood off shore again."

(Cook's name of Cape North was later reversed to North Cape. On today's maps it is *Mys Shmidta*, or Cape Schmidt, a change made by the Russians during the 1930's to honor their explorer, Otto Schmidt.)

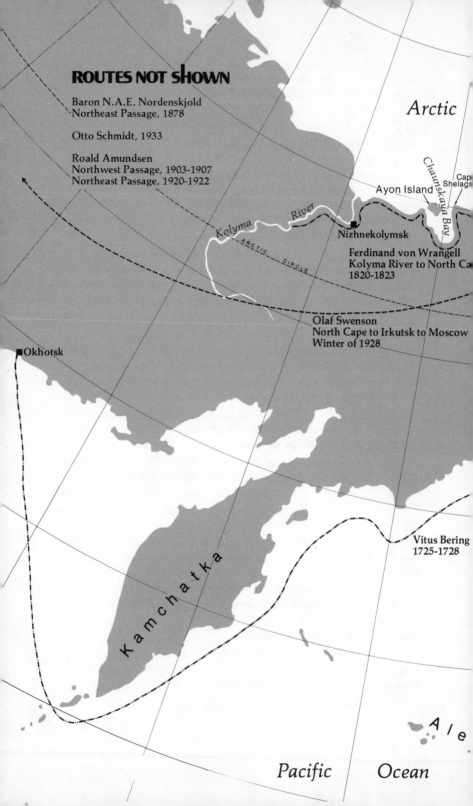

ROUTES NOT SHOWN

Baron N.A.E. Nordenskjold
Northeast Passage, 1878

Otto Schmidt, 1933

Roald Amundsen
Northwest Passage, 1903-1907
Northeast Passage, 1920-1922

Arctic

Chaunskaya Bay

Cap
Shelag

Ayon Island

Kolyma River

ARCTIC CIRCLE

Nizhnekolymsk

Ferdinand von Wrangell
Kolyma River to North Ca
1820-1823

Olaf Swenson
North Cape to Irkutsk to Moscow
Winter of 1928

■Okhotsk

Vitus Bering
1725-1728

Kamchatka

A l e

Pacific   Ocean

EXPLORATION OF THE ARCTIC

'cean

Icy Cape

North Cape
(*Mys Shmidta*)

Cape Lisburne
Point Hope

Chukchi Sea

ARCTIC CIRCLE

Fairbanks

Cape
Serdtse-Kamen'

*Kolyuchin
Bay*

York
Mountains

Seward
Peninsula

East Cape
(*Mys Dezhneva*)

Saint Lawrence Bay

Diomede Islands

■**Teller**

Bering Strait

■**Nome**

Cape
Prince of
Wales

Bering Sea

Bristol Bay

Dutch Harbor
■

Unimak Pass

**Captain James Cook
1775-1779**

Islands

an

With the sea almost free of ice, Cook continued southeast along the coast, rounded East Cape, explored further in the Bering Sea and, after a difficult passage through the Aleutian Island chain, went on to winter in the Hawaiian Islands which he had discovered earlier on this same voyage. There James Cook, probably the greatest and most humanitarian explorer the world has known, fell a victim to tragic mistakes in communication with the generally friendly Hawaiians and was killed.

Long before Cook had reached North Cape, the Russians were coming down the rivers of Siberia and exploring their Arctic coast, but no one had gotten much to the east of the great Kolyma River's mouth. Ten years after Cook reached North Cape, Catherine the Great approved plans to survey the coast from the Kolyma to East Cape. Her first expedition, under Joseph Billings, an Englishman who had served with Cook, failed miserably.

In 1820, Lieutenant Ferdinand von Wrangell, in charge of a new attempt to make the survey, decided to do it during the winter by sled, rather than trying to sail the ice-choked sea. The first year he made it from the Kolyma to Cape Shelagskiy before turning back. Three years later he was able to get down the coast to North Cape, at last proving to Europeans what the Eskimos had known from centuries of trade, that there was no isthmus stretching northward to America. Much later, Admiral Baron von Wrangell was a director of the Russian-American Trading Company and Governor of Alaska.

The Siberian Arctic coast we are concerned with, from East Cape to the Kolyma River, is by air only a little more than 800 miles long. At East Cape are high steep bluffs rising directly from the sea and three mountain peaks close behind them. Just around East Cape, the typical shoreline for the Arctic coast begins, with gentle slopes, sandy beaches and many lagoons. All the way west to the Kolyma River there are only a few prominent coastal features.

Cape Serdtse-Kamen', 90 miles northwest of East Cape, is a rocky bluff. Past the obscured entrance to Kolyuchin Bay and 300 miles onward, almost exactly on the 180th Meridian, is North Cape, which is very prominent with its rocks several hundred feet high. The cape is connected to the shore by a thin, long sandspit tied to a low rocky bluff a mile east, with a shallow crescent-shaped bay between, exactly as discerned by Cook. From North Cape it is almost 300 miles to Cape Shelagskiy, which again consists of high rocky bluffs and is the most northerly part of this coast. From

Shelagskiy to the Kolyma River, the coast is again mostly low land and tundra, featured only by Chaunskaya Bay and Ayon Island. All along the coast the hills are not far away, unlike much of the North Slope of Alaska where the tundra often stretches a hundred miles inland.

Arctic Ocean currents make this coast one of the most difficult to traverse by ship, with the ice always close on shore even in a good summer. When Baron N.A.E. Nordenskjöld made the first northeast passage in 1878 in the *Vega*, he was caught by the ice in September and forced to winter. And even in 1933, the famed Soviet arctic explorer Otto Schmidt (after whom North Cape has now been named) was caught off this coast and his ship, the *Chelyuskin*, was crushed in the ice and lost. Fortunately, all the crew were taken ashore by airplanes from Alaska.

With this description of the inhospitable Siberian coast, beginning 50 miles across Bering Strait from the nearest point in Alaska and 170 miles from Nome, we'll go to the story of the *Nanuk* on her last trip to Siberia.

NANUK–FROM SEATTLE INTO THE BERING SEA

CHAPTER 2

THAT THE *NANUK* WAS IN THE ARCTIC, AND especially the Siberian Arctic in 1929, was due to the enterprise of Olaf Swenson. Swenson was born of Swedish parents in Manistee, Michigan, in 1883. He accompanied his father in the gold rush to Nome, and in 1902 they went on to Siberia, still searching for gold. Their small boat was dismasted in a storm in Bering Strait, and they eventually wintered in Siberia. With this Arctic background, Swenson established his first fur trading post in

1904. He gradually developed a thriving business which continued almost without interruption until the Russian revolution resulted in termination of his work and confiscation of his trading posts.

But with his knowledge of Siberia, its natives and their language, and the comparative ease of transporting needed goods from Alaska or Seattle to Siberia, Swenson was in a position to negotiate further arrangements for the valuable fur of the region. In 1926 he formed the Swenson Fur Trading Company, and after great effort and much time spent in Russia (he spoke Russian, too), he entered into a joint trading venture with the Soviet government. The 5-year contract provided that Swenson would obtain American merchandise in accordance with Soviet specifications to be delivered to Siberian villages, and the U.S.S.R. would turn over to Swenson the fur collected in the territory to be sold in the U.S.A., with the Swenson company receiving a percentage of the sales. Many years later Swenson wrote that "during this period the Soviets lived up to their contracts meticulously."

To fulfill the initial contract, Swenson prepared in Seattle to make a trip each year through Bering Strait and a thousand miles northwestward up the Arctic coast of Siberia to Nizhnekolymsk on the Kolyma River. For this purpose he bought the schooner *Nanuk* from the Northern Whaling and Trading Company of Seattle.

In 1926, and again in 1927, *Nanuk* made Arctic trips through open ice without incident, each trip taking only about three months.

But 1928 was very different. Swenson had obtained an additional contract and needed a second ship. To find one suitable for ice work in time for the 1928 season, he went to Norway and there purchased the schooner *Elisif*, which set sail at once for Seattle (by way of the Panama Canal) under the Norwegian flag. Her captain was Even Larsen, of Brevik, Norway. In Seattle, she took on cargo and was fitted with a radiotelegraph transmitter. Captain Jochimsen, ice pilot, and Charles Huntley, radio operator, joined the Norwegian crew. Olaf Swenson and Ray Pollister, a business associate of Swenson, also sailed in their new (old) ship. The *Nanuk* accompanied them.

Ice conditions north of Bering Strait in the Chukchi Sea in 1928 were very bad. After several weeks trying to work her way through the ice, *Nanuk*'s propeller was severely damaged and she returned to Seattle under sail. Enroute home, much of her cargo was unloaded at Teller, Alaska, to be stored until the next summer.

By the end of August, 1928, the *Elisif* had made her way only as far as North Cape. She became fast in the ice trying to round the cape and was frozen in there in the open sea, about three miles northwest of the cape. All but Swenson spent the winter on the ship. He made a 4,500-mile trip by dogsled and deersled to Irkutsk, Siberia, in the dead of winter. From there he took the Trans-Siberian Railroad to Moscow, eventually reaching New York and Seattle, which is another story.

The winter of 1928-1929 on the *Elisif* was rough because of her exposed position in the ocean ice pack. The wireless proved of tremendous value. They communicated almost daily with the U.S. Army Signal Corps station at Nome and through the connecting Army system to Fairbanks and Seattle, and then via commercial systems into homes in Norway and to the government in Moscow. The ship's radio was the only means of communications on the Siberian coast.

**Charles A. Huntley and the schooner *Elisif*, frozen-in
at North Cape on the previous season's voyage. The photos
are from March of 1929.**

Through the radio, negotiations were carried on with Moscow to obtain permission for flights from Alaska, and with owners of commercial aircraft in Alaska to make such flights. Lack of good aviation gasoline was a problem, as well as the hazard of flying 450 miles of an almost uninhabited coast to land on ice hummocked with hard-packed snow. Noel Wien, one of the pioneer Alaskan pilots, with a new Hamilton cabin monoplane on skis, finally agreed to make the trip from Fairbanks to Nome to North Cape. After waiting several days at Nome for good weather, Wien and Calvin Cripe made the flight on March 7, 1929.

The landing strip was even worse than they feared, and the all-metal single-engine aircraft barely missed severe damage in landing. Furthermore, the gasoline turned out to be even lower grade than expected, and they were able to take off with only a partial load of fur the next day. However, the weather was good all the way back to Nome.

The thought of more trips that winter was eliminated by the Russians' termination of permission. Permission was renewed in October, 1929, and the same aircraft made two more flights to the ship.

Because 1928 ice conditions in this part of the Arctic were so severe compared to 1926 and 1927, there was some reason to expect that 1929 might be better. Swenson hoped the *Elisif* would be freed from the ice in early July, to proceed westward to her original destination, the Kolyma River, and return safely. The *Nanuk* would visit Saint Lawrence Bay, East Cape, Cape Serdtse-Kamen', North Cape, Chaunskaya Bay and Nizhnekolymsk, about 100 miles up the Kolyma River.

In the spring the *Nanuk* was overhauled, and Swenson decided to have a radio station aboard. Although I did not know it then, I was to be the radio operator—"Sparks," as wireless operators at sea were nicknamed.

Born in Seattle and raised with the romance of shipping and the sea about me, I had already worked three springs and summers in Alaska as a radio operator—first with the U.S. Army Corps of Engineers in Wrangell Narrows and in 1927 and 1928 at the Kake salmon cannery. People would ask me about the Arctic, but in three years I had been only as far north as Juneau. I decided that for my final trip after my junior year in college (I was studying electrical engineering at the University of Washington) I would go to Point Barrow if possible. Charles Huntley, radio operator on the *Elisif*, was an old friend, and through his parents I learned that the *Nanuk* would make another trip and would be equipped with radio. The radio equipment was being installed by the Radiomarine Corporation of America, so I had to apply to them for the job. I got it—$115 per month and "found" (room and board).

The *Nanuk* was built in 1892 in Eureka, California (on the spit, at what was then called Fairhaven), by the renowned schooner builder, Hans Bendixsen. This little schooner, built for his own use, was christened *Ottilie Fjord*. In 1923 she was sold to the Northern Whaling and Trading Company and later renamed *Nanuk*, the Eskimo name for the polar bear. For work in the Arctic ice, *Nanuk*'s hull was sheathed with two inches of Australian ironbark. A diesel engine was installed, and a crow's nest for observation and navigation in the ice was placed high on the mainmast.

I first saw the *Nanuk* at Lake Union Dry Dock, Seattle. Even up on the chocks she did not look very big—261 tons, 120 feet long, three-masted, schooner rigged, with a small, low cabin and the wheel aft. Her crow's nest and new radio antenna distinguished her topside, and a big, 200-horsepower, six-cylinder, Atlas Imperial diesel engine below.

Aboard the *Nanuk* I met Captain R. H. Weeding, a small, dour man who had been in the Arctic with Swenson before. The crew was not yet assembled; most had not yet been hired.

To install the radio, one of the four staterooms opening into the after cabin saloon had been used, with the converted spark transmitter (RCA ET3628, output 500 watts) and a small wall desk for the receiver occupying most of the space. There was just room for my typewriter and my chair. For power, I found that I must depend on a very old two-cylinder make-and-break-ignition gas engine coupled to a 220-volt DC generator which also was used for the winch (to raise sails, anchors, and handle cargo), for the main pump, and for charging the ship's 32-volt batteries. An undesirable complication was that power for the filaments of the two big transmitter tubes came from this old set of batteries, which were primarily used for lighting. *Nanuk*'s radio call letters were WKDB.

Like all radios used in ocean shipping at that time, *Nanuk*'s transmitter operated on wavelengths of 600 meters—the international distress and calling channel—and longer. A 600-meter wavelength is equivalent to a frequency of 500 kilohertz.

This was long-wave radio, based on frequencies lower than the 550- to 1,600-kilohertz range of the AM broadcast band. Long waves travel well horizontally, through water and over the earth's curvature, a reason for also calling them ground waves.

In the early 1920's, the value of short-wave transmission was realized. It was discovered that short waves could be bounced off the ionosphere (sky waves) and transmitted great distances. By 1929, many ham operators were working in the new short wave.

I had had auxiliary short-wave equipment at the Kake cannery in 1928, but the marine radio companies did not normally furnish such equipment for ships. As a radio amateur (since 1923) I had been most anxious to have a short-wave transmitter aboard for long-distance communication. Recent new federal regulations had made it possible for radio amateurs to operate their portable stations aboard U.S. ships, but only while in U.S. ports. For this purpose I brought aboard the *Nanuk* a short-wave receiver, parts for a 40-meter transmitter, and a 32/400-volt dynamotor to use with my portable license (call K7ABF; my home amateur call was 7OY.) By the time we were in the Bering Sea, I had the little 5-watt transmitter built on a breadboard and mounted vertically on the bulkhead under the radio room desk.

While I was still in school the *Nanuk* was taken through the locks from the lake to Puget Sound and around to the Bell Street Terminal on Elliott Bay. The radio was tested (a serious fault in the transmitter installation was corrected) and other preparations for sailing were completed. We took on diesel fuel for the main engine, gasoline for the auxiliary engine, and coal for the stoves; we later deeply regretted having no aviation gasoline.

The cargo included everything from flour and tea, through canned goods, clothing, clothing material, tobacco and candy, to small arms ammunition and 380 cases of dynamite, which were loaded from the launch *Dupont* as we departed Puget Sound.

We left the evening of June 15, 1929. The next day we passed Cape Flattery; all sails were set, and we headed for Unimak Pass in the Aleutians. Making very good time with strong northeast winds the last several days, we sighted the mountains of the Aleutian Islands on the 25th, went easily through Unimak Pass, and docked at Dutch Harbor with the U.S. Coast Guard cutter *Haida* at noon on June 26. This first leg of the trip had given most of those aboard their first good look at one another. All the crew had been called to the saloon the day before sailing to sign on. I was a little surprised to note that the duration of the voyage was stated clearly as 19 months, not the 3 or 4 we all planned, but no one balked.

Top—Unalaska, across from Dutch Harbor, on the way north.

Bottom—*Nanuk* and U.S. Coast Guard cutter *Haida*
at Dutch Harbor, June 26, 1929.

Although Captain Weeding had sailed for Swenson before, he had never wintered in the Arctic. The chief engineer, Bill Bissner, was a real Arctic veteran; he was a man about 60, wise, wizened and tough. Bissner had been with Swenson, afloat and ashore, for many years. His assistant, George Hunter, about 35, had made several Arctic trips.

The balance of the crew appeared to have been picked up almost haphazardly by Captain Weeding; certainly little thought had been given as to how they might meld under difficult conditions. Holmstrom, first mate, was a big Swede with a wild temper and no arctic experience. Arnold Draven, second mate, was a young man of German extraction. Of the four sailors, two had never been on a sailing ship—one German, one Irish, one Finn, and one black sheep from a good New England family. Although RCA had hired me, I was responsible directly to the captain.

Clarke Crichton was the cook and steward, and had talked Weeding into letting his son, Clarke, Jr., 15 years old, come along as cabin boy.

We also had a supercargo, Tzaret Berdieff, a recently Americanized Russian, who acted as clerk and interpreter. He was to keep tally on deliveries and the fur to be picked up.

Then, of course, there was Olaf Swenson and, surprisingly, his daughter Marion, 17. Of his two daughters, Marion was the one who very much wanted to participate in her father's adventures. She was signed on as a cadet.

Opening off the saloon in the after cabin, the three small staterooms quartered Marion, her father, and Captain Weeding. There was a companionway aft to the stern and a door forward to the main companionway and to the mess room. Flanking the mess room, four small rooms provided bunks for the mates, the engineers, the two Crichtons, and Berdieff and me. Forward of the mess room on the starboard side was the galley, while the port side opened into and down to the engine room. The forecastle for the four sailors was a small house on deck just aft of the foremast.

The single hatch into the hold was located just forward of the mainmast. In addition to the cargo below and on deck, four barges for cargo delivery were nested on deck, along with a small double-ended launch and a pram. Two whale-boats were slung outboard from davits alongside the cabin.

We left Dutch Harbor late on June 26, running into rough seas as we came out of the bay, and we pitched and rolled heavily

Marion Swenson, on the voyage north.

during the night. The Bering Sea was now mostly free of ice, and the steamer *Victoria* had already been able to reach Nome. On the 29th, we saw Nunivak Island to the east with the mountains still snow-covered. Our knowledgeable skipper stopped the ship, and in about an hour we had caught three barrels of codfish. The wind had ceased and the water was rippleless with almost no swells, so all sails were taken down and we proceeded on the engine alone, with which the *Nanuk* made about 6½ knots.

Nanuk under way north—first to Alaska, and then to Siberia—in June, 1929.

SIBERIA, NOME &TELLER

East Cape (*Mys Dezhneva*)
Diomede Islands
Cape Prince of Wales

men'

Sewar

York
Mountains Pen'

■Teller

■Nome

Bering Strait

Port
Clarence

Norton
Sound

CHAPTER 3

ON JUNE 30, WE ROUNDED SAINT LAWRENCE Island and headed for our first stop in Siberia, Saint Lawrence Bay just south of Bering Strait. At this latitude the sun set about 11 p.m. and we saw it go down behind the distant mountains of Siberia ahead of us.

We were awakened at 5 a.m. by the jarring and grinding of the ship as she hit small pieces of ice—a new experience for me and most of the crew. We were in thick fog with drift ice all around us

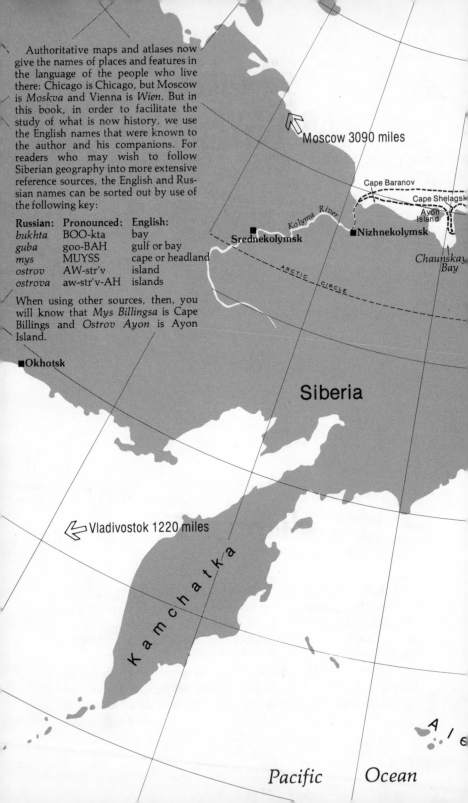

Authoritative maps and atlases now give the names of places and features in the language of the people who live there: Chicago is Chicago, but Moscow is *Moskva* and Vienna is *Wien*. But in this book, in order to facilitate the study of what is now history, we use the English names that were known to the author and his companions. For readers who may wish to follow Siberian geography into more extensive reference sources, the English and Russian names can be sorted out by use of the following key:

Russian:	Pronounced:	English:
bukhta	BOO-kta	bay
guba	goo-BAH	gulf or bay
mys	MUYSS	cape or headland
ostrov	AW-str'v	island
ostrova	aw-str'v-AH	islands

When using other sources, then, you will know that *Mys Billingsa* is Cape Billings and *Ostrov Ayon* is Ayon Island.

Moscow 3090 miles

Cape Baranov

Cape Shelagsk

Ayon Island

Srednekolymsk

Nizhnekolymsk

Kolyma River

ARCTIC CIRCLE

Chaunskay Bay

■Okhotsk

Siberia

Vladivostok 1220 miles

K a m c h a t k a

Pacific   Ocean

A l e

VOYAGE of NANUK
JUNE 15, 1929 TO AUGUST 2, 1930

Arctic Ocean

⇑ Spitsbergen 1960 miles

Wrangel Island

Icy Cape ←

Cape Billings

**Icebound at North Cape
October 4, 1929 to
July 8, 1930**

Cape Lisburne
Point Hope

orth Cape (*Mys Shmidta*)

ARCTIC CIRCLE

Fairbanks
Winnipeg 1970 miles ⇒

Cape Vankarem

East Cape (*Mys Dezhneva*)
Diomede Islands
Cape Prince of Wales

Cape Serdtse-Kamen'

Amguema River   Kolyuchin Bay

Territory of Alaska

Uelen
Dezhnev
Lavrentiya ■

York Mountains
Seward Peninsula

■ **Nulato**

■ **Teller**

Saint Lawrence Bay

Port Clarence

■ **Nome**

■ **Unalakleet**

◄Anadyr'

Bering Strait

Norton Sound

Saint Michael ■

Anchorage ■

Providence Bay

U.S.S.R.
UNITED STATES

Saint Lawrence Island

Bering Sea

Nunivak Island

Bristol Bay

Saint Paul Island

Seattle 1590 miles ⇒

Unimak Pass

Dutch Harbor ■
Unalaska

ian   **Islands**

and the Captain was threading the ship through the ice in the fog. After a couple of hours, the fog cleared suddenly and we found ourselves a few miles off the entrance to Saint Lawrence Bay.

As we proceeded into the bay, which was free of ice, we saw the new Russian village of Lavrentiya. It consisted of several heavily built wooden houses, a school and a hospital. Swenson hailed a large native skin boat and Swenson, Berdieff, Marion and I got in and were paddled shoreward. On reaching the beach we were greeted by the Russian agent and his wife and some others. They first made us line up and took a picture of us, and then we were introduced all around—in Russian of course, Marion and I not understanding a word.

I hunted up the radio operator and found him with the gas engine operator, two pleasant young chaps. The radio equipment and power plant were housed in one small building and the transmitter was quite interesting, 500 watts, a very haywire-looking rig but it seemed to work into Anadyr' on about 49 meters; they had no long-wave transmitter or receiver for communications on the international marine frequencies.

When we got back to the *Nanuk*, we found that the Chukchi Eskimos were all over the ship, although not below deck. They certainly were a curious lot, and they stared at us as though we were museum pieces, especially Marion, who was followed about continually. This was my first acquaintance with the Chukchis—or any Eskimos—and I found them most interesting. They were very friendly, and even jovial, strong and wiry, though appearing bulky in the parkas which they wore even in the summer weather. I saw Bill Bissner in happy conversation with two of the young men, then he brought out two new Winchester .30-30 carbines and two cases of ammunition and gave them to the men, who were obviously delighted. I was told that these were two of Bill's sons, and that he had spent many winters at Saint Lawrence Bay. Later I learned that for the Alaska-Yukon Exposition in Seattle in 1909, Bissner had brought his and two other families, with their huts, sleds, dogs, harpoons and all, and they had lived on the exposition grounds. The wet winter and civilization proved to be hard on them, with much illness, and Bill took them back to Siberia as early as possible the next summer.

We pulled anchor and headed for East Cape at 5 p.m., traveling on a smooth sea quite close to the cape's rugged bluffs and could see Big Diomede Island (U.S.S.R.) looming up to the north-

Top—Settlement at Lavrentiya, Saint Lawrence Bay, Siberia.

Left—The gas-engine operator and the radio operator at Lavrentiya.

Right—The radio station.

Top—Approaching East Cape (left); Big Diomede Island
is dead ahead.

Center—The cliffs of East Cape.

Bottom—Eskimos look down the engine-room hatch at
Nanuk's big six-cylinder Atlas diesel engine.

east near the center of Bering Strait. (Today the cape is *Mys Dezhneva* and Big Diomede is *Ostrov Ratmanova*.)

I was now able to communicate with Chuck Huntley on the *Elisif* 350 miles away, with signals becoming excellent as we rounded East Cape. Pollister and Swenson exchanged greetings; Pollister said they were eating only old dried spuds, seal liver, rice and fish ducks, so step on it! Swenson advised him that nothing was healthier than seal liver. The *Elisif* was still frozen in solidly.

This communication was, of course, by radiotelegraph. Neither ship had radiotelephone equipment, but to Chuck and me, both good telegraphers, key work was almost like a personal conversation.

On rounding East Cape we were in that part of the Arctic Ocean called the Chukchi Sea. We had to tie up to the ice off the village of Uelen, as the inner part of the little bay was still solid ice. Presently two dog teams and sledges came bumping out over the rough ice, with three Russians and about twenty Eskimos. After much talk we found that the Russian high official we needed to check in with was not there, but was at Dezhnev, 17 miles back on the south side of East Cape. We started back around the cape.

We arrived at Dezhnev around 6 a.m., and after waiting four or five hours, the Russians appeared, one a soldier in uniform with rifle and bayonet. We proceeded to Uelen again with the Russian official and the soldier. After another three-hour delay at Uelen, we started northwest up the coast, headed for Cape Serdtse-Kamen' where a great deal of fur had been gathered. The plan was for the *Nanuk* to take the fur to Nome for shipment to Seattle before we went on up the coast to meet the *Elisif.*

Our trip up the coast to Cape Serdtse-Kamen' was uneventful but, here too, the shore ice had not yet broken away and the fur had to be sledged out to the ship. After picking up the fur, we dropped the Russians back at Uelen and headed for Nome. With the beautiful weather continuing, we arrived there on the morning of July 5.

The Nome left from the gold rush days was scattered all over, with a few battered plank roads and some good dirt ones. The town appeared to be dying, to judge by the many deserted buildings, but, even so seemed prosperous because of several gold dredges working nearby. I visited the Army radio station briefly and saw operators Joe Drummond and Jack Dowd who handled much of the communications with the *Nanuk.*

Nanuk in the Arctic Ocean, July, 1929.

Top—Chukchi Village on the cliff at East Cape.

Bottom—At Cape Serdtse-Kamen', bringing out the fur.

Then I was put to work labeling fur sacks for shipment to Seattle. They were mainly white fox, with some ermine, and their value was placed at $340,000. In the evening we left for Teller and anchored in the bay there at noon the next day. The crew loaded and shifted cargo around all afternoon and I had a lot of contact with a Russian steamship, the *Stavropol*, which was en route to the Arctic from Vladivostok. I also worked radio amateurs in San Diego and Honolulu with my little short wave ham transmitter and had messages relayed home.

There was much less snow and ice at Teller than on the Siberian side, and the hills were beginning to get green. There was a reindeer meat packing plant and quite a number of white people, and they didn't greet us with guns either. The single operator of the Army station was J. H. Anderson; he had only a 50-watt long-wave transmitter, but with a very large and high antenna, so his station got out well.

off for NORTH CAPE

chapter 5

AT LAST WE WERE READY TO START UP THE coast to North Cape and the *Elisif*, then to go on together to our final destination—Nizhnekolymsk.

With the excellent weather continuing, we left Teller on the 8th, very heavily loaded. The man at the wheel could not see over the flour piled high on the main deck, and the stern was low in the water. We crossed Bering Strait easily, stopped at Uelen to reenter Soviet waters, and began the Siberian voyage we came for.

We neophytes aboard thought that even though the *Elisif* had reported no breakup of the ice, the ice would soon clear and we would push on smoothly as we had been doing in these calm seas. The Arctic veterans knew better; they knew that there were summers when ships could not reach North Cape at all.

The Arctic Ocean ice pack, some of it probably centuries old, is a permanent covering of the sea, constantly in slow motion with the winds, winter and summer. This year's ice mixes with last year's and many winters before that. Even in mid-winter the movement produces cracks and large stretches of open water called leads. As the leads close, backed by pressure from hundreds of miles of pack ice, the edges crumble and ridges are formed 30, 40, and even 50 feet in height, producing in effect small icebergs, some extending a hundred feet below the surface, all frozen into a massive conglomeration. The most powerful ice breakers cannot work against the pack, as the oil companies who built the tanker *Manhattan* to take oil from the North Slope of Alaska found out. The huge vessel was trapped by ice in M'Clure Strait and barely got out with the help of the Canadian icebreaker *John A. Macdonald*.

The *Nanuk* could, of course, buck none of this pack pressure but with her engine could readily go down narrow leads and through slack ice. Most important, her shallow draft permitted her to work close to shore, inside of grounded ice which would protect her from the main pack when the wind was not directly onshore.

Even before we reached Cape Serdtse-Kamen', we ran into heavy ice where the sea had been clear before. There was so much fog we could not tell how far offshore we were, which made it hard work for the captain or mate, the man at the wheel, and the engineer on watch. Continuous bells and signals came from the captain or mate who stood on an improvised bridge atop our deck load of flour, waving their arms for direction and pulling a long cord to the engine-room bell. Fog prevented use of the crow's nest.

When we were traveling in ice in clear weather, the captain would go aloft 80 feet to the crow's nest and signal the engine room with an electric bell system while the man at the wheel craned his head upward to watch for arm signals on which way to turn and how much.

For two days and nights we made only fair progress, and then were stopped by impenetrable ice not far west of Cape Serdtse-Kamen', about 18 miles offshore. (Here, just east of

Top—The Russian steamship *Kolyma,* which had wintered near Ayon Island, receives coal from *Stavropol* at North Cape for her trip south.

Bottom—*Elisif, Nanuk* and a Russian Junkers 233 floatplane off North Cape at the beginning of August.

Kolyuchin Bay, the Swedish expedition ship *Vega*, making the first northeast passage, was frozen in the ice from September 28, 1878, to July 18, 1879.) It was decided to turn back and try to find a lead along the edge of the shore ice. We were able to get inside the main pack and ran along well in shallow water for some hours, but eventually the lead forced us offshore again until we had to stop about 3 a.m. on July 12. We expected wind or current soon would open the pack for us, but we barely moved for 17 days.

During this time, the *Nanuk* was in considerable danger several times. On the third day, the wind shifted to the east, and as the pack began to move along the edge of the shore ice, a very large and heavy piece caught on the point below us and swung toward the side of the ship. With the tremendous force of the entire pack behind it, this was no place for us. We managed to push forward with the moving ice, around another point of the shore ice, and got a stern line out on a huge solid looking mass, perhaps 30 feet high.

While we were tying up the bow, the high piece astern broke away and began to sink into the sea. I was aft, helping to push off small pieces with a pike pole, and as we stood there we saw a great green-colored surface rising slowly out of the depths. The berg was turning over on its side, and the part which had been underneath was coming up under us. Swenson said in a tense voice, "There goes our rudder!" It cleared the rudder by a foot.

In the next few days we were forced to move several times to escape vast moving floes. Luckily *Nanuk* was able to take evasive action and sustained no real damage. The only thing we did other than ice work was to take on fresh water which we pumped from pools on top of ice floes. After so many bucket baths, I decided to go swimming and dove off the side. The shock of the 36-degree water was like getting hit in the head with a plank.

The worst thing was just waiting, day after day. Swenson said to me repeatedly, "The Arctic will teach you patience!" but even he began to get grumpy under the strain of his worries. He complained about how much gas I was using to run the transmitter for my schedules with Nome and the *Elisif*. The huge first mate was obnoxious as hell, and little Crichton, the cook, finally chased him out of the galley with a cleaver. Old Bill Bissner took to carrying a 10-inch wrench in his back pocket, and he warned me to look out for the mate, too.

During this long waiting period, besides handling all messages with Nome and the *Elisif*, I began to work regularly with the Russian steamer *Stavropol* which had rounded East Cape and was making her way up the Arctic coast. In addition to the *Stavropol*, we knew that the Russian steamer *Kolyma* had wintered near Ayon Island and would soon be heading south, and that a Russian icebreaker, the *Litke*, was scheduled to come up later and go to Wrangel Island, directly north of North Cape.

At last, with a bang, on July 28 things started to happen. Shortly after midnight the wind shifted and the bay in which we were located began to close up. We needed to move to a larger hole, and in a hurry. A huge square floe, perhaps three or four miles on a side, was closing in fast from the east. We headed between it and the section to which we had been tied up but prospects did not look good. Marion was on deck with only slippers on her feet, and her father sent her below to put on mukluks and pack her bag. If we got caught in the bottle neck it would be goodbye ship.

We made it through, and as the day went on, the wind picked up strong from the east, loosening the ice pack around us rapidly.

The wind was also strong from the east at North Cape, and on the 29th the *Elisif* reported it was free after being icebound 11 long months. Chuck said it was just a gradual break-up without danger, and that they were now anchored near shore to wait for us.

Big leads opened in the ice around us and soon we were on our way, running at full speed much of the time. The day was beautiful and the sea smooth. As we continued, a great mirage developed. It looked as though there was a big cliff of ice, miles away and hundreds of feet high, all around us except on the shore side. Although we appeared to be hemmed in by a vertical ice barrier, we actually were going along at full speed about a mile from shore, with five or six miles of flat country along the beach, gradually rising to a range of mountains that paralleled the coastline.

At last we rounded North Cape (*Mys Shmidta* on today's maps) and anchored near the *Elisif* on the western side about a quarter-mile from the beach. *Elisif* was a wonderful sight to us, as *Nanuk* no doubt was to the other crew. Shortly a launch pulled out from shore, went to the *Elisif*, and then headed for the *Nanuk*. I hardly recognized Chuck in the bow of the launch. His hair was bleached white and his eyebrows were dark, which gave him a peculiar appearance. I won't attempt to describe how I felt when he jumped on deck—it was great to see him, that's all. Huntley and I

STORY OF TRAVEL IN ARCTIC IS TOLD BY SEATTLE GIRL

Marion Swenson, Broadway High School Student, Radios Details of Russian Flyers' Visit to Colony.

Marion Swenson, seventeen-year-old Broadway High School girl with the Olaf Swenson expedition to the Siberian Arctic, sent her story to The Times by wireless and cable via Nome, Alaska.

By MARION SWENSON.

ABOARD THE MOTORSHIP NANUK, OFF CAPE NORTH, Arctic Siberia, Saturday, Aug. 3.— Accompanied by the Norwegian motorship Elisif, which was imprisoned in the ice for a year, we are proceeding westward to the Kolyma River. Even away up here in the bleak Arctic wastes, you hear the roar of the airplane. The Russian Junker 233, the type of plane used by Baron von Huenefeld during his transatlantic flight, arrived at Cape North July 29.

The plane carried three famous Russian airmen, Krashinsky, Valvitca and Leongard. The aviators and their plane were transported from Vladivostok to Lawrence Bay, where they started their flight. They visited Wrangell Island and returned to Cape North, reporting that a colony of seven Russians, including three women and a girl, ten years old, and fifty Chuchas were on the island.

Island Is Hunters' Paradise.

All the inhabitants of the little dot of land off the Siberian Coast are well, according to the Russian aviators. They still have eighteen months provisions on the island.

A soviet ice-breaker is now bound from Vladivostok to Wrangell Island, having been ordered there by government officials at Moscow.

After visiting us, the Russian aviators proceeded for the Kolyma River, the New Siberian Islands, the mouth of the Lena River, to Yaktuska and Irkutsk.

Frozen Seas Loose Grip On Schooner

Ice Breaks And Elisif Sails Again, While Rescuer Is Marooned

THE auxiliary schooner Elisif of Seattle, which was frozen in Arctic ice while en route to the Kolyma River, Siberia, in July, 1928, finally broke loose yesterday and resumed its long delayed trip to trading posts.

But the rescue ship Nanuk, which left June 16 of this year to carry relief to the Elisif, is frozen in. She is expected to break loose with a few more days of warm sun.

Aboard the Elisif is Charles Huntley of Seattle, radio operator, and on the Nanuk his Roosevelt High School chum, Robert Gleason. They had planned a happy meeting when the two ships met. Gleason is radio operator on his ship.

The Elisif will return to Seattle the latter part of September, if she does not encounter further trouble.

It was July 1, 1928, that the Elisif set out for Siberia.

Then came the long winter months, with no hope of getting loose before summer.

Elisif steams into the bay at North Cape, August 1.

had been firm friends since the second grade of grammar school. While in the Boy Scouts we became interested in telegraphy and radio, and went on to get our amateur and then commercial licenses. Our friendship continued through many years of airline communications work together, until his death in 1968.

We delivered much of our heavy load and I checked freight until 10 p.m. Then Chuck and I sat up until 3:30 a.m. talking. After listening to him, I hoped more than ever that the *Nanuk* would not be caught like the *Elisif*.

While we were unloading, the Russian seaplane that had flown from North Cape to Wrangel Island that morning glided in out of the north. It was a small, single-engine German Junkers 233 on floats. The plane carried three Russian airmen—Krashinsky,

Russian Junkers 233 floatplane at North Cape, August 1.

Valvitca and Leongard—who were famous at that time. The next morning they soared away for Kolyma. We envied their capability.

On August 2 (we skipped a day to the Siberian date and time at North Cape) a strong northwest wind came up about 4 a.m. We pulled out and picked our way back around to the east side of North Cape to escape ice moving in from the north. The *Elisif* could not get started in time and was now stuck in a very bad position if the wind should increase. We were in the little bay between North Cape and its adjacent headland, anchored in about three fathoms with grounded ice on the seaward side to protect us from the main pack.

We damned the wind! If it had not been for the wind, both ships would have been well on the way to the Kolyma.

At this time Swenson sent a big news article to the Associated Press about the plane flying to Wrangel Island. We knew it would be published in Seattle, and the folks at home would know that the *Nanuk* had reached North Cape and the *Elisif* and all was well.

While we were waiting for the pack to open again, Marion, Chuck and I climbed up to the top of North Cape. Everywhere the ice was solid as far as the eye could reach. A desolate, bleak, but awe-inspiring sight.

The Russian steamer *Kolyma*, which had been frozen in a hundred miles northwest of the Cape, reported that she also was now free and making her way slowly down the coast. The Russian steamer *Stavropol* was only 12 miles east of us but held fast by the ice; some of her crew walked up the beach to the cape while we were waiting.

After six days, the ice at last began to loosen up seaward. I went up on the cape again on the 8th and could see the *Kolyma* about 15 miles out to the westward. The *Stavropol* had moved a couple of miles closer from the east. The *Elisif* was able to move around the Cape and anchor in the bay near us that afternoon. That night Swenson, Pollister, and the two captains held a conference on the *Nanuk* and decided that both ships would up anchor and try to sail out at 4 the next morning.

The next morning the *Stavropol* anchored near us, but we left and rounded the cape with the *Elisif* right behind us. Then we saw the *Kolyma* coming in, so we both anchored to wait and have a confab on conditions to the westward. Next the *Stavropol* came around the point, and all four ships anchored together at North Cape.

Top—At North Cape, supplies from the *Nanuk* are unloaded with an *umiak* and a launch. Assistant engineer George Hunter stands on the bow of the launch.

Bottom—A Native village on the beach; North Cape is in the distance, to the west.

Top—The Russian steamship *Stavropol* at North Cape
in early August.

Bottom—*Elisif* at anchor in the bay at North Cape,
two days before she foundered.

THE WRECK of THE Elisif

CHAPTER 5

THE LAST VOYAGE OF THE *ELISIF* BEGAN AT 11 a.m. August 9, 1929, as she started up the coast from North Cape. About an hour later, the *Nanuk* followed her.

We passed the *Elisif* about 3 p.m. because the *Nanuk* drew less water and the going was best close inshore. Being smaller than the *Elisif*, the *Nanuk* could maneuver more readily; by midnight the *Elisif* was not in sight. The going was pretty fair, as an east wind had come up and was helping to open up the ice.

The assistant engineer got pie-eyed that evening on some vodka from the *Stavropol*, and the chief broke me in on the engine. I stood watch alone a couple of hours, and there were plenty of bells in the ice work. The diesel engine was directly connected to the propeller without a reverse gear—it ran backwards for reverse—and it was started on compressed air. There was one drawback. When the *Nanuk* was under way and an order to reverse came through, the propeller kept the engine turning—forward—for some time. After you had cut off the fuel and reset the valve lever to reverse, you had to stand there waiting for the big flywheel to stop before it was possible to give the engine the compressed air to start in reverse. At four bells and a jingle—full speed reverse and hurry—it seemed the flywheel would never stop.

After 24 hours we were still going strong, almost 100 miles beyond North Cape, but the going became more difficult as we pushed westward. The wind swung to the west and began to rise. The *Elisif* was having a bad time 30 miles behind us and radioed that they would have to tie up, but Swenson told them to "try their damnedest" to keep coming, no matter how much the ship got banged around—and they did.

The wind was increasing all the time and the current was getting stronger; *Nanuk* was running directly into both.

At 6 p.m. on August 10, we rounded the lowland at Cape Billings and found plenty of ice ahead; also the wind grew stronger—a full gale—and it began to snow hard. We turned back, found a large grounded ice cake just off the cape and, after much difficulty, tied up to it. We watched the situation closely because the line might pull loose or the cake break up at any time. The *Elisif* came through and found a place to anchor about five miles behind us.

Next morning there was still a strong gale blowing, but it had stopped snowing. The wind had swept the snow clear of the decks but the masts and rigging were pretty well caked up with it. The hills were covered with a fine new coat of snow and looked beautiful—but cold!

We let go of the ground ice we were tied to and went out to take a look at things even though the current and wind were still strong. After we had run five or six miles the pack started closing toward the beach again but we found we could keep going. I wired the *Elisif* to that effect, and they decided to follow. We agreed to listen for each other every two hours and swap information.

At 2 p.m. I worked Chuck again. We were going along all right with quite a bit of open water, although we could see that it was not so good ahead of us.

Chuck had cleared Nome at noon, and he sent one message for me because I was having difficulty receiving Nome because of noise from the engine. It was the last time he worked Nome.

Just before 4 p.m., five miles west of Cape Billings, we struck a very bad strip of grounded ice and loose floes wedged tightly together by the strong west wind, still blowing right at us. We got through this 400-foot stretch after more than an hour's work. It was the worst time we had had yet. Several times it looked as though we were stuck hard. As fast as we pushed ahead a little, the wind and current would force the ice in around us, especially at the stern where one hard bump could break the propeller or rudder or both. The propeller hit twice, but again we were lucky and no damage resulted.

At 6 o'clock I started the auxiliary engine and sent a message to Chuck, telling him about this bad strip and that there was plenty of open water ahead. I asked him to start up at 8 o'clock and let us know how he was coming. After listening a bit, I cut the receiver and went on deck to help fend off ice at the stern.

We hit another bad spot about 7:15 and had to go into three fathoms, which gave us about three feet clearance to get through it.

A few minutes before 8 p.m. I went down and started the engine. I switched on the receiver.

What I heard was, "SOS, SOS, WKDB from LCYB. For God's sake, Bob, please come on! If you don't answer this time, will send blind."

I started the transmitter generator, threw on the filaments and yelled at Marion, who was sitting in the after cabin, to get her father quick.

I answered Chuck, told him I was with him, go ahead. He came back quickly, said they were beached. Dynamo in water, power likely to go any second. He shot me three messages to the effect that the ship was sinking and had been beached at 7:30 p.m.. Swenson sent one telling Pollister to take plenty of provisions ashore and we would have the Russian steamer *Stavropol* pick them up. Chuck said crew was in no danger, ship still on level keel, and to send wire home for him.

Pollister told us not to come back to where they were beached, but I do not think we could have anyhow because the ice had closed in behind us. We were in open water, proceeding full speed for Chaunskaya Bay. There was no protection along the coast where we were.

Chuck was sending perfectly. We talked for about twenty minutes, expecting every minute that his power would go as the water had reached the generator. It finally did, but not before we had received all the necessary information. As his power went off, it was the end of radio station LCYB.

Chuck said that at 6:30 they had struck a floating cake, no harder than they had hit some before, but at 7 p.m., when the engineer made his regular check, he found water rising rapidly in the hold. The ship was sinking, having opened a seam in her stem (at the point of the bow). At 7:15 the captain authorized an SOS and Chuck finally got the Russian ice breaker *Litke*, which was in the ice pack about 45 miles south of Wrangel Island. He had much difficulty working with him but got through some information he was to relay to us. Chuck also had been calling me and sending SOS for 45 minutes while I was standing on deck. It must have been hell.

It was a sad end for the *Elisif*; frozen in all winter and then cracked up so soon after they at last were freed.

The next question was: How was I going to get this information to the outside? It was too late to get Nome that day, and next day was Sunday in America so Nome would not be on. The U.S. Coast Guard cutter *Northland* was way down south at Saint Michael. I worked the *Litke* and he told us that the *Elisif* had "sent SOS, was crushed in the ice and cast on the beach." No one else had heard the SOS.

The first thing was to catch the *Stavropol* before it passed Cape Billings and ask it to stop for *Elisif*'s crew. *Litke*'s operator and I continued to call the *Stavropol* but her operator was not on watch. I called Nome and the *Northland*—full power and then some—until 10 p.m. but nothing doing, so I cut the engine to wait until dark, when reception would be at its best. I continued listening. It was a good night, fairly dark in spite of the clear weather, and signals began to roll in.

About midnight I got the cutter *Haida*, somewhere in the Bering Sea, and told him there had been an SOS in the Arctic and that I had important messages. He got the Saint Paul Island Navy station in the Pribilof Islands to call me. After I sent Swenson's message to notify his Seattle office and all officials and families concerned, and one to Chuck's folks, Saint Paul quit on me to relay

SEATTLE SHIP, ELISIF, BEACHED IN ARCTIC SEAS

No Lives Lost as Ice-Crippled Vessel Driven Ashore to Prevent Foundering, Radio Message Reveals.

CASTAWAYS on the bleak shore of Arctic Siberia, 300 miles east of the Kolyma River, where their ship was beached to prevent foundering, twenty men, officers and members of the crew of the Norwegian motor vessel Elisif of the Swenson Fur Trading Company of Seattle today were awaiting the arrival of a rescue ship, the Russian freighter Stavatoll.

First news of the wreck was received in Seattle at 7:30 a. m. yesterday by Clyde M. Huntley, 6555 19th Ave. N. E., father of Charles (Chuck) Huntley, 21-year-old wireless operator of the ill-fated vessel.

The message, which came from Bob Gleason, young Huntley's chum, who is radio operator of the Swenson trader Nanuk of Seattle, follows:

Text of Radio Message.

"Elisif wrecked three hours ago. Talked with Chuck by wireless until after ship was beached. Absolutely all are in no danger. Russian steamer will pick them up tonight or tomorrow. They have plenty of provisions ashore. Fine weather."

The Elisif sailed from Seattle July 10, 1928, for the Siberian Arctic with a cargo of trading supplies. She is commanded by Capt. Even Larsen of Brevik, Norway, who came with the vessel from Europe. R. S. Pollister of Seattle, a representative of the Swenson Fur Trading Company, also was aboard the wrecked vessel.

Olaf Swenson, president of the trading company, and his daughter, Miss Marion Swenson, 17-year-old Broadway High School girl, are aboard the Nanuk, which sent the news of the disaster to Seattle.

"I am sure Chuck will come out all right," said Mr. Huntley. "Following his graduation from Roosevelt High School he was not very strong and decided to go to sea in search of health. He made one voyage on the steamship W. M. Tupper from Seattle to the Kuskokwim River district of Alaska and became very fond of seafaring. He has been quite a student of radio and had a set of his own with him on the ship.

Ice Believed Responsible.

"The news of the wreck was a surprise to me, for Saturday night we received a wireless message from Chuck saying they were about 300 miles from the Kolyma River and all well. When the Nanuk sailed from Seattle June 16 we sent a lot of Christmas presents and things to Chuck to be sure he would have a pleasant time on the holiday. I suppose they were all lost in the wreck. Chuck is just 21 years old and 6 feet tall. I believe the Elisif was damaged in the ice and had to be beached. The message from the Nanuk came via the radio station on St. Paul Island in Bering Sea."

The Elisif is a three-masted motorship. She arrived in Seattle June 27, 1928, from Brevik, Norway, via Newcastle-on-Tyne. The vessel was brought to Seattle by Capt. Nils Larsen and his son, Capt. Even Larsen, who commanded the vessel on her ill-fated voyage. The father returned to Norway via New York soon after the arrival of the ship here.

The Elisif formerly operated as a North Sea trader and in the coastwise routes in Norway. She was purchased in Brevik in 1927 by Mr. Swenson, who at that time was touring Europe. The vessel came here from Norway with a crew of thirteen men, who, with other seafarers, were aboard when she was beached.

Had Been Ice Captive.

The wreck of the Elisif came after she had been freed from a year's imprisonment in the Arctic ice off North Cape, Siberia. She escaped from the ice in July and had resumed her voyage to the westward in the Siberian Arctic. Saturday night the Elisif was caught in the ice again and so badly damaged that she had to be beached to prevent sinking.

They Play R·

HERE are fourteen members of the crew of the fur schooner Elisif, which was wrecked Saturday on the Siberian Coast. The crew of twenty is now safe

inson Crusoe

on a lonely beach. The accompanying photograph was taken while the Elisif was "frozen in" north of the Arctic Circle.

BEACHED CREW AWAITING BOAT

First direct word from the wrecked Seattle trading schooner Elisif, on the beach at Cape Billings, on the Siberian Coast, was received here last night.

It was a wireless from Charles Huntley, radioman on the schooner, to his parents, Mr. and Mrs. C. M. Huntley, 6555 Nineteenth Avenue Northeast. It read:

"Elisif stove by ice. Beached Cape Billings. Transmission disabled by engine room flooding, but receiving O. K. How's everybody?

"Returning via motorboat to Nome shortly. Expect me October. Nothing to worry about. Love and cheerio all."

After being imprisoned in the ice for a year, the Elisif broke loose recently, but began leaking badly when open water was reached, according to information received by B. Roy Anderson, marine broker here.

Radio dispatches from the coast guard cutter Northland, now in Bering waters, last night stated that it had received word that the crew of twenty were safe. Supercargo R. S. Pollister asked the Northland to proceed to East Cape, Siberia, and pick up the crew there, the Northland's message stated. The Elisif survivors will make their way to East Cape either in their own small boats or by the Russian steamer Stavatoll, which is now en route to Cape Billings.

water line, and had filled rapidly. They certainly were lucky that they were able to get in to the beach with her—and that there was a beach. On many occasions both ships had had miles of heavy rough ice between them and the shore.

As the *Stavropol* continued to stand by, we were told that none of *Elisif*'s crew were willing to continue on into the Arctic with the Russian ship. Most of them wanted to take their small boats and try to work their way back to East Cape. Some would stay to salvage cargo until the *Nanuk* returned.

Then *Elisif*'s captain advised us that the crew refused to stand by the *Elisif*—they had had enough of Arctic Siberia. By 7 p.m. it was decided that the entire crew and Pollister, 20 men in all, would take their two launches and two loading barges and start for East Cape at once. We were to advise U.S. authorities and arrange for the cutter *Northland* to pick them up at Uelen September 1, by which date they hoped they could traverse the 500 miles of coast. I hated to sign off with Chuck. Here we were, still trying to get to the Kolyma and back, and Chuck's crew were embarking on a hazardous trip in open boats. The outlook was not good for either of us.

We were still unable to move, and my communication difficulties were increasing. With only low frequencies and 500 watts of power, I was having a hard time reaching Nome in daylight, and the Nome Army station would not open at midnight for the special schedules I requested. I could still work the *Stavropol*, of course, but he was unable to get the nearest Russian stations, at Anadyr' and Srednekolymsk. The *Stavropol* had only a spark transmitter on long waves.

The *Stavropol* worked her way up to a point only 65 miles east of us but we still could not move. Considerable unrest arose among the crew, and the first mate began to campaign openly for "giving a man a chance to get out." Some wanted to start back in our launch. Captain Weeding told them he would give them a chance if things did not open up in a few days.

Swenson told me he thought we still had a fifty-fifty chance of getting out. There was no thought of turning back without reaching Nizhnekolymsk. I was not getting cold feet, but I was beginning to realize we might have to winter somewhere on this coast.

Being unable to communicate with the outside at all on my ship's transmitter, and understanding that we could desperately need that communication, I decided to try my amateur transmitter. I turned on the little dynamotor and soon established communication on 40 meters with another amateur station. I was using the call X7DD; his was X7XOT. He was the operator on the steamship *Wisconsin* bound from Portland, Oregon, to Shanghai. His position was "1,826 miles from the Columbia River," which put him about 1,500 miles south-southeast of us, near the Aleutian Chain. Using my ship's call letters on the amateur band, I gave him my official messages which he relayed to the Saint Paul Island Navy station on the marine frequencies.

Although we were still unable to move westward around Cape Shelagskiy, the most northerly point on our trip, the *Stavropol* worked her way up and anchored near us. The Russian radio operator, Baburin, came over to the *Nanuk* and brought me a letter from Chuck. We managed to carry on some conversation without Swenson's or Berdieff's interpretive help. *Stavropol* was just a small steel steamship, but she looked great to us. It was good to have company—even Russian-speaking company.

On top of everything else, we were short of gasoline for the auxiliary engine, with only six barrels remaining. This would last barely a month at the rate we were using it. There would be no use of my staying the winter without gasoline, but Swenson assured me there were 100 barrels on the *Elisif* if we could get it.

With tension on the ship becoming worse daily and new ice now forming on the calm sea, life was not pleasant but we continued to wait and to hope. All we needed was a favorable wind to open the ice pack.

At last, on the 17th of August, the ice opened a bit and the *Nanuk* and the *Stavropol* started westward again. The *Stavropol* soon gave up. We continued to wriggle and twist our way along, making two miles in five hours. Then a heavy fog came down, and we could move no more. Swenson came to the radio room and gave me the cheerful information that if we did not get out of this spot quickly, we would probably be stuck in the pack for the winter. We were far into an almost solid mass of ice which he thought would drift as a whole rather than break up, and the wind was now blowing hard from the north.

As the day went on the gale shifted a little to the east and began to open cracks in the ice. It was very cold, and a half-inch of new ice had formed between the floes. The only water visible was in the new cracks. Despite the wind, the sea remained flat.

Early on the 18th we reached more open water and began to travel almost continually under one bell (slow speed). Then the fog which had persisted in the gale suddenly lifted and we found we were around Cape Shelagskiy in open water near the entrance to Chaunskaya Bay. We soon picked up some Eskimos at the bay entrance and with their help, proceeded into this large almost uncharted bay to the village.

This village, like most we had seen, consisted of some half dozen native skin homes and a sheet-metal-covered Russian post building. The village was near the beach at the foot of some low mountains. The bay itself was about 30 miles long, bordered on one side by low mountains and gravel beaches and on the other by low bluffs, deeply eroded by the waters of melting snows—all treeless and bushless.

We rushed everything to take advantage of the open water, dumping our cargo on the beach, regardless of the agent's protests, and leaving about 9 p.m.

As we were moving out, we ran aground near the middle of the bay, at least two miles from the nearest land. With the bow now light, the ship had grounded at the stern and the bow would swing a little either way. We tried to work the *Nanuk* off by swinging, but sand got into the engine cooling system so we had to go easy. We put up two jib sails and with their help swung about 15 degrees but were still stuck. Then we moved four tons of lead (for bullets) from the lazarette to the foredeck by hand. Still no go. Finally we loaded an anchor in a barge, towed it to deep water with the launch, dumped it over, and at last kedged off the shoal. We were aground only about four hours but it took another hour to stow the sails, stow the lead and raise the boats. Then we were off to Kolyma again. We were lucky it was only a sand bar, because we had hit it at full speed. As expected, the sea was open outside the bay's mouth and we pressed on at full speed about 10 miles off shore with the ice three or four miles still further out.

Not having gone into Chaunskaya Bay, the *Stavropol* was now 10 miles ahead of us as we passed Ayon Island, where Roald Amundsen wintered when he made his northeast passage, 1920-1922. Amundsen, the greatest of all the polar explorers, had been the first to make the north*west* passage, which he did in the *Gjoa*, 1903-1907. With his northeast passage in the *Maude*, he became the first man to navigate a ship over the tops of both continents.

We went on, sometimes in fairly heavy ice, sometimes in fog, sometimes in both, but at last reached Cape Baranov only about 40 miles from the mouth of the Kolyma River. As we neared the river mouth, a small dirty-looking power boat met us. After much discussion about the depth of the water and the advisability of lightering cargo, we started up the river with a native pilot aboard and the small boat proceeding ahead. According to the soundings, we had about six inches clearance for half a mile over the bar. We had passed the *Stavropol* but she came up as we were crossing the bar. We had beaten her to the Kolyma by an hour and a half.

Soon after we crossed the bar it became quite dark even though the weather was clear. We could see the redness of the sunset on one side and the tip of a big red moon sticking up over the hills on the other. It was beautiful but we knew winter was near.

Instead of an early start up-river, we spent hours lightering 20 tons of the *Elisif*'s cargo from the *Stavropol*, anchored on the

**Russians lighter supplies up the Kolyma River from
Stavropol. The load included 20 tons of cargo
from the beached *Elisif*.**

other side of the bar. Then we started up the river. Our pilot was a skinny old fellow who spoke only Russian. I could not tell whether he was a Native or a Russian—perhaps a mixture. The river mouth was miles wide with many channels but this man took us up a channel without difficulty.

The river appeared to me as large as the Columbia, which divides the states of Washington and Oregon, but it was hard to judge its size because there were no trees or houses on its banks. The country surrounding it was broad, flat land or tundra, like all the rest we had seen; farther back, and occasionally along the river's edge, there were rolling hills and low mountains. The hills and mountains were never rocky or rough, but of gently contoured shapes. The only vegetation was thick brown grass, slightly green in spots. There was no snow to be seen anywhere, nor ice either, except the wall of ice we knew was behind us at sea.

As we continued at our best speed up the river, darkness caught us. There was not a cloud in the sky and we again had that phenomenon of sunset and darkest night at the same time. The northern half of the sky was light, almost yellow in color, and the horizon colored red by the sunset, while the southern sky was dark with a big full moon just over the eastern horizon and stars twinkling in the dark portion of the sky. The air was so extremely clear it seemed you could reach out and touch the moon or some of the brighter stars.

As the sky finally lightened and we resumed full speed, we saw trees on the land for the first time since we had left the Washington coast. They looked to be small evergreens, perhaps spruce, but it was hard to judge their size.

On the 23rd of August, we arrived at the end of our journey, the town of Nizhnekolymsk. Even at 4 a.m. the entire population appeared to be on the river bank to greet us—perhaps 300 people. We anchored 200 yards off shore, ran in a line and began unloading the cargo we had brought for the U.S.S.R. from Seattle.

Despite our fervent desire to start back at the earliest moment possible, we were not ready to leave until three days had passed. Even with the help of the villagers, unloading onto their small temporary dock was difficult and there was not only our cargo but that brought from the *Elisif*. Next, the *Stavropol* arrived and there was an equal urgency to unload her as fast as possible.

I could not reach Nome at all during the daylight and the only thing that was preserving our connection with the U.S.A was

Top—The cargoes of both *Nanuk* and *Stavropol* are
unloaded by small boat at Nizhnekolymsk. The return cargo
on *Nanuk* is $1 million in furs.

Bottom—Nizhnekolymsk, population 300. This settlement
consists of a church and a few homes, all heavily built of
wood. Many of the inhabitants are exiles of the czars.

my daily communication with that wonderful operator on the *Wisconsin*, both of us operating illegally on the amateur 40-meter band. I also contacted other amateurs in Seward, in Hawaii and in Tokyo. Infrequently, around midnight, I was able to reach the cutter *Northland* in the Bering Sea on my RCA transmitter on long wave. Radio conditions generally were excellent on both long and short wave.

One day after we quit work I decided to go swimming again. I was very dirty, the sun was warm and the river not very cold. However, I made a mistake in diving off the ship near the stern, not realizing how much current there was, and I barely made it back to the ship. I could easily have made it ashore by drifting downriver a way, but it surely would have been an embarrassed American landing in a Russian Arctic village in the cut-off trousers which served as my swimming trunks.

I was anxious to look around ashore and at last Swenson took me on a visit. The village consisted of one old church that was being used as a stable for six cows, a few small government buildings, and many small, rectangular flat-roofed houses. All were made of small logs or hand-hewed square timbers. There were no streets, the houses being set at any angle or position, and paths wound about among the houses.

A Russian policeman accompanied us everywhere. This was 1929, and everyone was suspicious of everyone, harmless though we must be. Despite our guard, two of the Russians invited us into their houses for black bread, fish and tea. That appeared to be all they ate. Their little houses were spotlessly clean but crudely furnished. Swenson told Marion and me that this village was made up mostly of people and their families exiled by Czarist regimes. Certainly they were most gracious, fine featured and well mannered, obviously not of rough peasant breeding. I wished we could get them out of there and have often wondered what happened to them as the Russian revolution further digested Siberia. Even Swenson did not know what their prospects were and did not ask in the presence of our police guard.

On the 27th, we loaded a huge cargo of fur with an estimated value of $1 million, also a large number of mammoth ivory tusks, and were finally ready to go in the afternoon. Then it began to snow hard, putting off departure until morning. A northwest wind also increased the possibility of ice at the river's mouth.

As we prepared to leave, the ship's winch motor, which had

been giving trouble handling cargo, burnt out its armature, so we had to lift the anchor with block and tackle; the 1892 deck windlass had long been beyond repair, with cogs rusted away. A good omen, however, was that I was at last able to work the Saint Paul Island radio station and the cutter *Northland*, which was at Nome preparing to go to East Cape to pick up the *Elisif*'s crew.

THE FATE of THE ELISIF'S CREW

ChAPTER 6

ABOUT 3 A.M. ON AUGUST 28, WE STARTED down the Kolyma river. The weather was clear and cold. The hills were covered with new snow, and looked much different than when we came up river only the week before. We worried about the ice to come.

After a fast trip, we made it across the bar as darkness came. In our launch we returned our pilot to his shack at the river mouth. The ice was not close in so we started eastward but it soon became too dark to risk navigation. We shut down and drifted for about four hours.

At dawn we started on, but soon after we passed Cape Baranov the pack pressed close to shore and we ran aground trying to go inside of it. We finally got loose, ran back to deep water, and tied up to grounded ice. I learned in this brief ice encounter how much more difficult ice work would be with the *Nanuk* empty of cargo and the stern now high in the water. Twice the propeller struck the ice hard.

The *Northland* reported that a severe southwest storm had prevented their going to East Cape and they were in the harbor at Teller waiting for the storm to abate. We had only a northwest breeze but it kept the ice in close around us. We hoped *Elisif*'s crew was safely at Uelen by this time but had no way of knowing.

After another day without progress, I got the *Northland* again and received very disconcerting news. The *Northland* had reached Uelen and found that the *Elisif*'s crew had started off for the Diomede Islands two days before. They were in the storm reported by the *Northland*.

On September 1, we tried to get through the ice off Ayon Island again but had to quit after our propeller repeatedly hit heavy ice and gave us considerable vibration aft. It looked bad. Swenson was organizing a group to pick up driftwood on the island's beach (there was plenty of it from the Kolyma's mouth) because we had coal for only 30 days more cooking.

That night the *Northland* told us that all the *Elisif*'s crew were safely aboard.

The plans for the cutter to pick them up at East Cape would have worked perfectly had it not been for the storm that began on the 28th. I had talked to the *Northland* that night, and they were already in a sheltered anchorage at Port Clarence, off the village of Teller. The *Northland* reported winds of Force 11 on the Beaufort scale, which is hurricane force. Ninety miles away in the Bering Strait, the *Elisif*'s crew were battling for their lives in open boats.

Captain Even Larsen, his Norwegian crew of 16 men and the three Americans who had spent the previous year with them (Ray Pollister, Swenson's business partner in the Swenson Fur Trading Company; Captain Jochimsen, the Arctic ice pilot; and my friend, Chuck Huntley, the ship's radio operator) had left the beach at Cape Billings on August 18. All 20 men, their personal belongings

Elisif lies aground at Cape Billings, August 11.
The men are salvaging supplies and preparing for the
trip south in the launches.

Elisif is fast aground and her boats are preparing to leave her.
Twice *Elisif* has been caught by the North, this time for good.

and enough gasoline for the 500-mile trip down the coast were loaded in two launches and two barges. The double-ended Norwegian launches were sturdy, and the men reinforced the bows with flattened gas cans to protect them from ice. One launch had a 15-horsepower engine, and the larger launch had 25 horsepower. The barges were those normally used for lightering cargo: large double-ended, flat-bottomed, dory-type boats about 30 feet long.

They struggled down the shoreline, sometimes making only a few miles in a day's work. They kept going five days and nights without rest, finally reaching the village of North Cape on the fifth day. The Russian official and the natives who had been with them throughout the *Elisif*'s wintering there welcomed them with open arms and helped in every way they could while the men rested for their trip on down the coast.

Taking advantage of open water and calm seas southeast of North Cape, they had then pushed on without stopping and reached the village of Uelen, on the north side of East Cape, on August 27. They had thought their battle was won. They were taken ashore to rest and recuperate, and to await arrival of the *Northland*.

At 2 a.m. on the 28th, they were awakened. The wind was increasing, ice was moving toward the shore, swells were developing, and their boats on the beach were in danger. They quickly got the boats off the beach and prepared to enter the lagoon, but the swells were already high on the bar at the entrance. They tried three times to get through the surf, but after nearly losing one barge with five men aboard they abandoned the attempt and decided to stay off shore until the weather moderated. They tried to find shelter in the lee of East Cape but could find none.

It was then decided to seek shelter behind Big Diomede Island, 20 miles away in the middle of the Strait. But even as they started, the storm increased in violence. As the seas grew higher, they twice snapped tow lines to the barges but managed to recover the barges and push on.

In a letter, Chuck Huntley later told their story.

"Finally reached point within five miles of Big Diomede only to have seeming victory snatched from us. The tow line of the big launch became entangled in its propeller and, with no steerage way, it was impossible to head into the sea and both launch and barge became partially swamped. In addition to this, the small launch was shipping seas and its engine running poorly

Elisif's crew start the 500-mile trip from Cape Billings to East Cape in open boats: two motor launches towing two double-ended, flat-bottomed barges.

FUR SHIP'S CREW BATTLES WAY TO SAFETY IN NORTH

One Barge After Another Abandoned in Stormy Voyage to Shelter Island in Bering Strait.

By Associated Press.

NOME, Alaska, Wednesday, Sept. 4.—The icy waters of the Arctic Ocean, crunching out the lives of ships on the bleak Siberian and Alaskan shores, took toll of another vessel three weeks ago, the motorship Elisif, but the crew of twenty baffled the northern storm king to arrive here with a tale of Arctic adventure typical of that found near the top of the world.

The flight from the wreck west of Cape Billings, Siberia, which occurred August 11, when the Elisif was stove in by the ice, was told by R. S. Pollister, agent of the Swenson Fur and Trading Company of New York, operators of the motorship.

"While working the ice just west of Cape Billings, Siberia, August 11, the Elisif was badly stove forward well below the water line," Pollister said. "She started to take water so fast that in spite of pumps both on deck and in the engine room, Capt. Edwin Larsen was forced to order the vessel beached."

Provisions Put Ashore.

Immediately after the vessel was beached, all provisions, coal, bedding and clothing for the crew were landed. On the morning of August 13 the steamship Staverapol, operated by the Russian Mercantile Company, arrived and anchored near the Elisif. About twenty tons of cargo was loaded on the Staverapol from the Elisif, and then the captain of the Russian vessel left, feeling that he could no longer detain his ship.

For five days, working eighteen hours a day, the crew with the aid of natives, lightened the remaining cargo.

"Shortly thereafter," Pollister continued, "the crew prepared two small barges and two launches for the trip to East Cape. The trip to North Cape, 110 miles, took five days. One night was spent at North Cape to rest the crew.

"The following day a start was made for East Cape. The trip was made under most favorable weather conditions. It was possible to run twenty-four hours a day, averaging 100 miles a day.

Aided by Russians.

"We arrived at East Cape the afternoon of August 26. The Russian officials invited the entire crew to live ashore and supplied quarters for them as far as they were available.

"Heavy swells started on the beach around East Cape the next day, and because of ice crowding on the beach it was necessary for the crew to take two launches and barges out to sea."

The troubles of the survivors then began again. They were unable to enter the lagoon at the Cape, and swells prevented them from finding shelter under the Cape. They finally decided to head across Bering Straits to Big Domede Island.

About ten miles off the Cape a southwest wind picked up. When they were only forty-five miles from the island a tow line between a launch and the barges parted. A new line was made fast, but it became fouled in the propeller of the more powerful launch, and heavy seas forced them to abandon one barge, as the small launch could not handle both.

Last Barge Abandoned.

The entire crew was taken aboard the remaining barge, the sea anchor put out and the launches rode easily during the storm until the morning of August 29. Heavy seas made it impossible to continue on with the barge to the island, and it also was abandoned. The crew was taken on board the two launches, which fought their way to Little Diomede Island. Landing was made at the native settlement through a heavy surf.

The next day the Northland appeared, picked up the crew and brought them here.

The Norwegian motorship Elisif sailed from Seattle last year for the Siberian Arctic on a fur-trading cruise for her owner, the Swenson Fur Trading Company of this city. She was frozen in at North Cape, Siberia, and spent the winter there. Her crew included Charles (Chuck) Huntley, wireless operator, son of Clyde M. Huntley, 6555 19th Ave. N. E.

SEATTLE TIMES

due to wet ignition. It was getting very dark and the wind was still increasing. The two launches and their tows became separated. The small launch was finally worked alongside its barge and seven men transferred into the launch. There was no chance to save personal effects as the barge swamped entirely as the last man left.

"Very dark, and heavy sea made it nearly impossible to locate the big launch and barge. After a heartbreaking search, we found them. The captain had fashioned a sea anchor to hold the big launch and barge into the wind and a man had gone over the side in the icy water and managed to untangle the tow rope from the propeller. We secured the small launch astern of the remaining barge and prepared as best we could to ride out the storm. The chief engineer and I bailed the small launch all night to keep her from sinking. Very cold and both frozen in spots. Entirely exhausted by daylight.

"Can remember very little of the next day and night. Sea very rough and did not expect to last it out. Sure found out why they say that Norway puts out the best sailors in the world. Some wonderful seamanship displayed.

"Morning of the 30th our water supply was exhausted. Sea calming considerably but found had drifted 60 or 70 miles in a northerly direction during the storm. Decided to abandon the barge and make a break for Little Diomede Island. All the men were crowded into the launches and everything in the barge abandoned.

"The sea was very rough for the overloaded launches but the engines kept running and we made it to the village on the western side of the island just before dark. We ran the launches through the heavy surf to the rocky beach with the help of all the Eskimos who had come down to meet us.

"For the first time in 14 months we were on American soil!

"I cannot adequately tell of the wonderful treatment we received at the village. The schoolhouse was thrown open to us and we were fed like kings.

"The very next day the *Northland* arrived off the village and picked us up. We again had a wonderful reception, and the warm hospitality of the entire ship's crew on our passage to Nome, arriving there September 2."

THE bATTLE bACK TO NORTH CAPE

chapter 7

THE *NANUK* WAS UNABLE TO MOVE FOR TWO more days, when at last the wind shifted to southeast and the ice began to slacken. As it did so, the *Stavropol* made its way up beside us—they, too, ready to battle down the coast. At 3 a.m. on September 3, we both rounded the tip of Ayon Island and headed for Cape Shelagskiy from which point the coastline begins a slight southerly trend.

With the *Stavropol* ahead of us—she was faster in open

water, and our banged-up propeller had reduced our speed to six knots—we went around Shelagskiy in a thick fog and strong wind. We passed within 150 yards of the cliffs and could just see their tops through the fog. Soon darkness forced us to anchor. At daybreak and in clear weather, we found that we had passed the *Stavropol* somewhere in the fog, and she was now four miles astern. Then, with open water and both ships running at full speed, the *Stavropol* soon passed us with much waving between our crews. With darkness and the appearance of some ice, we were again forced to tie up to grounded ice for the night. The *Stavropol* kept on (she had a searchlight; we did not) and eventually disappeared from our view.

With first light we were on our way again and reached the stranded *Elisif* about 6:30 a.m. We tied up to ice near the beach and rushed ashore to get all that we could. This included several drums of gasoline and kerosene, canned milk and what coal they had—only 15 sacks. I picked up two boxes of radio apparatus which Chuck had packed and left for me, and Swenson carefully retrieved all the kerosene lamps.

Swenson wanted someone to stay there to salvage more cargo. Jimmy Crooks, whom we picked up at Kolyma and who had wintered two years on this coast for Swenson, was glad to have the opportunity. Quite a character. He got Arnold Draven, our second mate, to stay with him, and they packed up and went ashore with Jimmy's dog team. Jimmy said he would visit us soon because he did not expect we would get far. We hoped he was wrong.

We also picked up the *Elisif*'s dog team and sled which they had used the previous winter. They had left them with the Eskimos who kept watch on the beached ship. Swenson was preparing for the worst, and we did not like the prospect.

As we moved down the coast, communications improved and I now worked Nome regularly again with the ship's transmitter. The *Stavropol* reported that with great difficulty they were still moving slowly toward North Cape. The *Northland* was staying at Nome, solely on our account.

By the 6th of September we were within sight of North Cape, about seven miles away. Here we were stopped by a great ice pack in against the Cape. The *Stavropol*, in trying to round the Cape, had become stuck fast in heavy ice about four miles ahead of us, three miles offshore. We were better off because we were still in open though shallow water, shoreward from the main pack. The

Stavropol was very near the spot where the *Elisif* had wintered.

We were again forced to wait for the ocean current to change, and the change would come only with a southerly or easterly wind to move and open the pack.

Meanwhile, *Elisif*'s crew was in Nome and the Army operators let Chuck work directly with me for an hour, using their big arc transmitter. Pollister and Jochimsen had left for Fairbanks by airplane in order to get to Seattle sooner, because the next steamship would not leave Nome for nearly three weeks. Chuck and the rest of the crew had to wait, but were happy in Nome. We wished we were there with them.

The icebreaker *Litke*, homeward bound from Wrangel Island and only 130 miles away, advised the captain of the *Stavropol* and our Captain Weeding that they could come to our assistance if necessary. Captain Milozorov advised the *Litke* that he expected to get around the cape all right and did not need assistance. We all wanted the *Litke* to come but Swenson and Weeding were compelled by Milozorov's reply to concede that we could also make it on our own. And Swenson told us that if the ice was packed hard by a northwester, even an icebreaker could not help us. He really knew the Arctic and the terrible strength of the pack.

Two days later, with a light northwest wind blowing and the ice filling in on the beach behind us, I heard the *Stavropol* operator come on and call the *Litke*, using the "urgent" call. We waited hours until he finally got the *Litke* and requested the icebreaker to come to their assistance. The *Litke*'s captain replied that he would request approval from his Moscow headquarters to return, which cheered us greatly. We didn't know that he apparently would never get approval.

Meanwhile, more days went by. We shifted around now and then, and once were within four miles of the cape but had to move back several miles to stay in open water. The *Stavropol* was unable to move at all. New ice was getting stronger every night and it began to look as though we would be forced to winter off this beach.

It became pretty tense on the ship, and the first mate beat up one of the sailors. Everyone, including Swenson, was trying to figure out what was going to happen, and what we would do if it didn't happen. We started using kerosene lamps exclusively and I held my engine use to the minimum. We were in a better position to winter than was the *Stavropol*, but not much. Because of Noel

Wien's flight in March, we knew we were within range of aircraft from Alaska and, although we had no aviation gas, we still felt aircraft could get most of us out.

On the 14th of September, after a night of light eastern winds, the ice began loosening up. By noon there was a lead outside of us extending all the way to and beyond North Cape. But between the *Nanuk* and the lead there was about two miles of pack, held together by new ice that refused to crack. The ice inshore had not broken either, and the *Stavropol* remained about in the middle of a large stretch of pack ice. By nightfall the situation had not changed.

Stavropol is caught in the ice pack, three miles offshore. This is near the spot where *Elisif* had been frozen-in the winter before.

The 15th dawned bright and clear but with still no change. Swenson wanted to try blasting out the strip between us and the open water right away. He brought up a case of dynamite and put it by the galley stove to thaw out, but Weeding decided to run back westward and try to find some opening into the lead, now wide and sparkling under the sun.

We went back about 15 miles through new ice, in some places two inches thick, and finally started into a somewhat broken path leading north. Then the damnable fog came in as we looked for openings to the east. We stopped and waited nearly three hours, then in desperation continued northward, taking a chance on getting into the big lead parallel to the coast that we had seen in the early morning.

At last we came to fairly open water and were able to move eastward again, but with the fog we did not know where we were. We kept the edge of the ice to starboard, knowing that if we were in the main lead we would soon come to North Cape. We ran along listening for sounds from the *Stavropol* and watching for the Cape, but saw and heard nothing until we almost ran into the headland bluffs across the bay from North Cape. We turned around, ran back a mile into the little bay between the Cape and the bluffs, and tied up to ground ice there.

Then the excitement began with the *Stavropol*. They had heard us go by outside them in the fog, and belatedly roused their operator to his transmitter. Captain Milozorov radioed us to please take the *Stavropol*'s 32 passengers. The ship could not move and he was sick in bed.

We could well imagine the consternation aboard the Russian ship. They thought we were sure to get out while they were held fast in the ice with all those passengers, including several women and children from Nizhnekolymsk. But we could not possibly take them all, and it was doubtful that we should take anyone, with our chances of reaching the Bering Sea still so slim. We lacked accommodations and had hardly enough food aboard for our own crew for the winter.

During the night I worked hard at my key with the slow Russian operator. Swenson and Weeding finally agreed to take 10 able men who could come aboard on condition that they bring their own bedding and food for three weeks and, if we got stuck, they would go ashore and hike back to the *Stavropol* or to the nearest native village. They were to be ready at six in the morning and we would pick them up from the ice as close as we could get to the *Stavropol*. Government officials aboard the *Stavropol* tried officially, and women appealed personally, asking that we take them, but we simply could not do it.

Swenson also went ashore, exchanged five of the *Elisif*'s dogs for better ones, and bought mukluks and reindeer skins for parkas—for all of us in case we had to winter down the coast.

Fate disregarded all our preparations. Before dawn, a northwest wind came up and the ice began closing in from the solid pack to the north. We did not move, and our radio message to the *Stavropol*, telling them we could not come, only made final what was already obvious to them. The great lead in which we had rounded North Cape the day before was closed. It looked as though we'd never make it out, although a few still felt that a southerly gale might again open the ice and permit us to escape.

Instead of southerly winds, they prevailed from the northwest, and the pack was knit tighter together by new ice every day. On the *Stavropol* they could do nothing. On the *Nanuk*, we moved about occasionally to stay in the remaining open water. But we began to prepare to winter. The sails were taken down and stored carefully below deck, leaving the ship looking mighty bleak. Swenson sent Eskimo dog teams back into the hills to procure reindeer from the "deer natives." These are the Natives who herd reindeer, live off them, and use them for transport. They stay back in the valleys among the hills where there is moss and other vegetation for the deer. When Swenson's party returned with three carcasses we were treated to fresh meat, which we found wonderful after months of salt beef.

The *Elisif*'s crew departed for Seattle on the last trip of the steamship *Victoria* on September 24, and I talked to Chuck for the last time as he used the *Victoria*'s transmitter. Then the *Northland* gave up on us and left Nome for Dutch Harbor. Despite all this, everyone remained in pretty good spirits, particularly me. I had had some flying experience and saw this little bay freezing over almost as smooth as a billiard table, with over a mile of clear ice into the prevailing wind. Swenson, from the ship, and Pollister (now in Seattle) had already begun initial negotiations regarding airplane transportation and there appeared to be several outfits who were interested, but some cooled when they learned that we had no aviation gasoline.

There were some ducks and geese still coming down the coast, and Swenson, Bissner, and I went after them every chance we got, using our little pram. One dawn we found the last little pool of water near us black with ducks. We crawled out over the ice and simultaneously fired, expecting to get several and have the rest fly off. But only a few were able to get away. Whether there was too much congestion or they were exhausted from a long flight I do not

Nanuk lies at anchor in the bay at North Cape, October 8, 1929. Here, 153 ducks were killed for food for the crew. Behind *Nanuk* is the last of the open water.

Top—The hills and mountains west of North Cape offer *Nanuk* some slight protection from the wind. *Stavropol*, lying exposed in the ice pack 3 miles northwest of North Cape, does not enjoy the same protection.

Bottom—Heavy grounded ice to the north protects *Nanuk* in the bay from the ice pack outside.

know, but we slaughtered 153 of them. We needed them, for us or for our dogs, because the winter was now almost upon us.

While *Nanuk* could still break through the new ice around her, we started the engine and drove the ship carefully into three inches of new ice as close behind North Cape as possible, headed to the northwest for maximum protection from the winter storms, and dropped an anchor through the ice. This was on October 4, 1929. *Nanuk* would not move again until July 8, 1930.

WiNTER AT NORTH CAPE

chAPTER 8

WE WERE ABLE TO USE A GANGWAY OFF THE
ship and walk ashore whenever we wished. The village on the beach
was about a half mile away; the steep slopes of North Cape were a
quarter-mile off our bow. To get to the *Stavropol* was a long walk
into and across the sand spit connecting the cape to the shore and
then out to sea three miles over very rough pack ice.

Demetri Miroshnishenko, the only Russian stationed at the
village, had been there two years. He was a pleasant young man

who spoke English quite well. Many of the Russian passengers on the *Stavropol* were members of a scientific expedition that had come down the Kolyma to Nizhnekolymsk. One of them was a medical doctor; he told us that Captain Milozorov was critically ill with pneumonia.

In our conversations with these men, either in fair English or with Swenson and Berdieff translating at times, we learned that some still leaned to the White forces but others were violently Red. It was only seven years since the Communists had taken over in Siberia. Swenson cautioned us to be most discreet, as we certainly wanted no trouble for the *Nanuk* here in Russian waters. But no one appeared to have any inclination other than to help each other in every way possible.

At the time, I had not realized the importance of having the *Nanuk* freeze in with her bow to the northwest. I was to learn during the winter of the fierce northwest gales which swept down the coastline. With her bow into these cold winds, *Nanuk* was far more livable than she would have been otherwise. The ship, of course, had no special insulation or accommodations for wintering, but Swenson with all his experience had made other important provisions.

A large tarpaulin was spread over the foremast boom and securely fastened at the sides and bow. This provided some additional shelter at the forecastle, covered the hatch, and provided sheltered working space on deck.

With lumber brought along for the purpose, a sturdy shack was built on deck over the main companionway, with a heavy door held tightly closed by weights on a rope over a pulley. An outhouse was built projecting over the starboard side of the ship with canvas top and sides. With the winds, this was a mighty cold place to visit; there were some who claimed to make it out and back before the shack's door slammed shut! (Marion used the head off the after cabin.)

The engineers, of course, had to winterize the entire ship, seal off all hull entrances, drain all pipes. The worst problem was to keep my gas engine running. This was before antifreeze coolants, so after cutting off the sea water, Bissner did it by first using a 50-gallon drum with salt water and, as the weather got colder, a 10-gallon drum. We had to watch it because if I ran too long we would boil the water out of the small drum.

We were running out of coal for our three stoves in the

Winter quarters. The outhouse is seen amidships,
projecting over the starboard rail, the galley smokepipe
behind it, the companionway shack to its left.

galley, forecastle and after cabin. This had been expected but we had ample diesel oil and Bill made up his patent burners to use the oil in the stoves. Five-gallon gas cans cut open at the top, were rigged with petcocks and lengths of copper tubing. The cans were hung on bulkheads near the stoves, with tubing run to the bottom of each stove. A few rocks were placed in the stoves just below the end of the tubing. The idea was to get the rocks hot enough to vaporize the oil dripping on them, but this was pretty tricky, with much smoke and soot developed in the process. I gradually inherited the job of caring for the after-cabin stove, which included running a chain down the stack to clear the soot each morning, starting the fire, and bringing in the oil. Many a day we had to ladle the oil out of the tanks, below deck in the side of the ship, because it was like molasses at very low temperatures.

To provide fresh water, the top was chiseled out of a 50-gallon drum which was carefully cleaned and placed in the galley near the stove. Blocks of ice were cut, hauled to the ship, and dumped in the drum to melt.

I had already learned that you can get fresh water from sea ice. If salt water ice is exposed to the air and evaporation, it eventually loses its salt. The trick is to find old ice that has not been redipped or covered with salt spray. Old ice looks a little clearer than new ice but a sure test is to make tea with it; if it is salty at all, the tea will taste sweet. There was plenty of suitable old ice grounded just north of the *Nanuk*.

The *Nanuk* was well provided with food for the winter, including dried fruit, tinned fish, and jams and jellies to prevent scurvy. Swenson also knew that almost anywhere on the coast you could go back in the hills and buy reindeer from the deer natives, as we had already done.

Further, the ship's slop chest was well stocked with heavy long drawers, wool socks, shirts, sweaters, pants and caps. The Seamen's Library had provided a chest of old books and magazines, most of which were to be read and reread during the winter. Among the books were Stefansson's *The Friendly Arctic* and Amundsen's two volumes, *The South Pole*. Marion had a small portable phonograph and 40 records.

The Chukchi Eskimos could be depended on to provide shelter and some food in an emergency but they had barely enough to eat themselves. They were always friendly, cheerful and anxious to help the strangers from the South in any way they could.

Nanuk crew members chop blocks of old ice
(that which has lost its salt) and haul the ice to the ship
by dog team for fresh water.

Top—Olaf Swenson stands with *Nanuk*'s dog team
on smooth ice. November, 1929.

Bottom—Clarke Crichton Jr., *Nanuk*'s 15-year-old cabin boy,
and his Eskimo friend, who is carrying a seal carcass.

One afternoon I paced off the clear flat ice to determine its size. A plane could land or take off on 700 yards of perfect ice in any direction in this bay, and there was an area a mile long and 500 yards wide pointed into the prevailing northwest winds. Aircraft could taxi right up to the *Nanuk*. Many passengers on the *Stavropol* wanted to go out by airplane, but there was nothing definite on planes or permits yet.

The Russians were worried about the *Stavropol* in her exposed position with nearly 80 persons aboard. Should a pressure ridge develop at the ship, she would surely be crushed. Although her bow had been strengthened for work in the ice, she was an ordinary old steel steamship, not an icebreaker. We understood she did have plenty of coal to keep her quarters warm all winter and still steam south the next summer.

One night on short wave I got in touch with Stanley Morgan, operator of the newly established Signal Corps station at Point Barrow. We found we could readily work our long-wave sets even though the distance was 560 miles. Teller also came through, so I had two alternates in case of any difficulty with Nome. We were working on the ground waves, traveling over an ideal salt water path, and signals were always good—night or day—regardless of ionospheric conditions.

An owner of an airplane reduced his price for several trips, which was hopeful. He had been quoting $700 per passenger, $3 per pound of fur, $4,200 each trip. Swenson told me that if they could get a reasonable price he would send out all the fur and most of the crew, perhaps even me on the last trip. Permits to make the flights had been requested some time ago, but there was no word of approval from Moscow.

Unexpectedly, Jimmy Crooks arrived from the *Elisif*. He reported that the vessel was frozen in without further damage and they were still getting cargo off her. His real reason for coming, however, was to ask Swenson to recall Draven; the two of them could not get along. Swenson agreed to do it, because Crooks was the best man for the job.

We were anxious for planes to come; almost everyone wanted to leave. The weather continued fair and our flying field had only a nice covering of about an inch of frost. Marion and I had been put to work with the sewing machine and shears, making small, box-shaped sacks into which we tightly packed the furs for air shipment; we had about 100 sacks ready.

Top—Russian engineers test the strength of the sea ice.

Bottom—These Chukchi boys are employed to cut ice around *Nanuk*'s rudder every day to prevent damage to the rudder if either the ship or the ice moves.

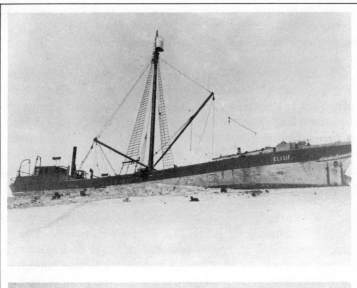

Top—*Elisif* in Siberia: spring, 1930. Jimmy Crooks has stayed with the ship since September to salvage the cargo, and that work has gone on through the winter. *Nanuk*'s second mate, Arnold Draven, had stayed with Crooks for a few weeks, but the two men didn't get along, and Draven left.

Bottom—The ice pack pushes up onto the beach near the village at North Cape.

We had been "anchored" now more than three weeks and everyone was unhappy at the lack of action. The first mate became even more obnoxious and rambunctious—only Swenson could handle him.

I went over to the *Stavropol* one afternoon and came close to not getting back. I had been invited alone for dinner and it turned out to be quite a party, with lots of toasts and singing and even the telling of many stories and jokes. The expedition meteorologist, George Kretschman, translated some of the stories for my benefit, and I learned that many jokes are international. The most elaborate story was one that I had heard before and have heard since in America.

The Russians delighted in drinking you down, which I well knew. By eating lots of food, I was able to stay with them even through the after-dinner drinks. They wanted me to remain on the ship, which made me all the more determined to go back to my ship. Around midnight I started out alone with a kerosene lantern.

The temperature was not too low and the sky was clear but there was a strong northwest wind blowing snow and obscuring the sky most of the time. I was following the dog team trail but the ice was very rough and about the third time I fell down, the lantern went out. I crawled behind some heavy ice and tried to relight it but could not. With the wind at my back, I knew I could make the shore unless I veered to the left and missed North Cape entirely. As a consequence, I kept too much to the right and finally hit the beach way west of the native village. I turned down the beach, and the first Chukchi hut I got to took me in, warm and safe. At daybreak I went on down the beach and out to the *Nanuk*. I never did sleep on the *Stavropol*.

There were eight native huts, called *yarangs*, in this village. Unlike Canadian or Alaskan Eskimos, the Chukchis do not move from winter to summer camps but use the same home the year around. Neither they nor the Alaskan Eskimos build igloos or even know how to build one. At North Cape their houses are built of driftwood, fairly round, about 20 feet in diameter, and domed-shaped, covered with walrus skins sewn together and weighted down with large rocks around the edges. The leeward side has a flap which serves as the entrance.

Inside, on a frame about 8 feet square and 4 feet high, is a room of deer skins which serves as the living room and bedroom. It is kept *hot* by seal oil lamps, without any ventilation. Part of the floor is covered with heavy skins, then deer skins in abundance which serve as the bed. The whole family sleeps in the nude together. The space between the inner sanctum and the outer walls is used as a storeroom for equipment, as housing for the dogs in a storm, and as a toilet. The smell of raw seal blubber, half-cooked food, and dirty bodies built up a stench which is almost unimaginable. Only in a storm could one be so grateful for refuge!

The Eskimo depended almost entirely on the sea for food even in winter, and starvation was never far away. But the village shared everything they had equally, even when one man got one seal. And they were always ready to give a visitor tea or any food they had that you would eat.

This classic igloo was built by the author; it is an object of curiosity to the local Eskimos, who do not make snow houses. The Chukchi Eskimos and their Alaskan counterparts build houses out of driftwood and either animal skins or sod. The Chukchi houses are round, built on the surface of the land, and covered with skins. Alaskan houses are rectangular, dug about three feet into the ground, and covered with sod. The dome-shaped house of snow blocks which is so often attributed to Eskimos is made by only one group of Eskimos, those who live along the arctic shore of Canada near the mouth of the Mackenzie River.

THE flIGHTS bEGIN

chApTER 9

AT LAST SWENSON CONCLUDED DEFINITE
arrangements with Alaskan Airways, a small company based in
Fairbanks, and the Russian government granted the permits. I
began to work Teller regularly because that would be the take-off
point, 450 airline miles from us. On October 26, a pilot named
Frank Dorbandt arrived in Teller with a Stinson Detroiter, a small,
single-engine, four-passenger, cabin biplane. He told us that Carl
Ben Eielson, the manager of the company, was coming with the

larger Hamilton monoplane, the one that Noel Wien had flown to the *Elisif* in March.

We heard from the Russians that the *Litke*, which had never come to our assistance, would bring two airplanes to Providence Bay on the Bering Sea about 350 miles southeast of us, and that they would take out the *Stavropol*'s women and children, and some of the men. Sixteen of the passengers were preparing to leave at once by dog team to meet the *Litke* at Providence Bay before the freezeup in the Bering Sea—a long tough trip.

Eielson did come to Nome from Fairbanks but damaged a landing gear strut landing there. Eielson told Dorbandt to go on alone while they repaired the Hamilton.

Wonderfully clear weather prevailed at both Teller and North Cape, so on the 29th Dorbandt took off. We, of course, told the others that a plane was on its way and soon everyone was gathered on the ice waiting and watching. It was 6 hours and 20 minutes before we first heard the Stinson's Wright Whirlwind engine and saw the speck in the sky—a real thrill for everyone, our link with the outside. Dorbandt's plane was on skis; it landed beautifully, and taxied right up to the *Nanuk*. As big Frank Dorbandt cut the engine and opened the door, we cheered. It was a great and happy occasion for all—Americans, Russians and Eskimos.

Dorbandt brought our mail, cigarettes and a case of coffee; no more, because the rest of his load consisted of gasoline for the return flight. He filed one message with me, to be sent to the Associated Press in New York—something like "Pioneer Alaskan Pilot Frank Dorbandt completed hazardous 6-hour 20-minute flight from Teller to North Cape in Stinson Detroiter to rescue *Nanuk*'s crew." In later years I was to learn more about Dorbandt's braggadocio, but on this night we loved him.

Dorbandt intended to go back the next day but Eielson had made quick repairs and Dorbandt told him not to change to skis. There was still little snow on the coast, and he could land almost anywhere on wheels. Dorbandt was to wait so they could fly back together. The next morning Eielson and his mechanic, Earl Borland, started for the *Nanuk*; their flight from Nome to North Cape took 4 hours and 20 minutes.

We had a great evening with these men. Eielson and Borland, contrasting with Dorbandt's loudness, were both quiet spoken, calm, and most pleasant. I remember particularly Eielson,

Top—Frank Dorbandt arrives at the *Nanuk* in a Stinson
Detroiter, October 30. The Stinson is a four-passenger
cabin biplane powered by a Wright Whirlwind engine.
On this flight, it carried mail, cigarettes, coffee—and
gasoline for the return flight to Teller.

Bottom—Carl Ben Eielson and Earl Borland land Eielson's
Hamilton monoplane at North Cape on October 31.
Their flight time from Nome was 4 hours 20 minutes.

Top—Pilots and *Nanuk* crewmen unload supplies from
Eielson's Hamilton. Captain R. H. Weeding is walking
toward the camera. Others, from left, are Marion Swenson
(only her back and head are visible) and her
father, Olaf Swenson, who are watching Frank Dorbandt,
a sailor named Hearn, Earl Borland and Carl Ben Eielson
(right) unload the airplane.

Bottom—Eielson and Borland warm up the
Hamilton to leave North Cape.

who had been a school teacher, producing a list of 10 words which he bet no one could spell, and my being proud that I spelled the most—eight—correctly. The only word I remember of the 10 was *sacrilegious*. We anticipated many more pleasant evenings together, realizing not at all that tragedy lay ahead.

The first day of November was clear but with heavy clouds on the eastern horizon and reports from Teller not very good. But they decided to start, and, if necessary, make a stop on the way. The planes had been loaded the night before. Dorbandt was to take four passengers and a small amount of fur, and Eielson the two heaviest passengers and about 1,000 pounds of fur. The Hamilton with her 425-hp Pratt & Whitney Wasp engine could take off with all the fur we could cram aboard.

Dorbandt's passengers were George Hunter, our second engineer; the two Crichtons; and Vic Johansen, a sailor. In the Hamilton were our troublesome first mate and Paddy, our demon Irishman. The hazards of the flight did not bother anyone. Everybody wanted to get out as soon as possible, except possibly Bill Bissner who did not seem to mind another winter in the Siberian Arctic. Swenson and the captain named who would go, except that in the case of the four seamen it was left up to them to decide which two would make the trip. The four men cut cards for it the night before departure.

Dorbandt took off first and Eielson followed a few minutes after, but returned to shut off his cabin heater because the cabin was getting too hot and he was afraid of damaging the fur. He got off again about a half hour after Dorbandt had left, at 10:10 a.m.

Neither plane reached Teller that night, and at 5 p.m. it began snowing hard there. No one worried much because we figured they had stopped along the coast at one of the native villages. The weather stayed bad at Teller for four days and it began to get foggy at North Cape. We were afraid the planes would not reach Nome in time to catch the last boat, the small motorship *Sierra*, but on the afternoon of the fourth day Dorbandt arrived at Teller and Eielson flew directly into Nome. Dorbandt changed to wheels and flew to Nome. Both planes came back to Teller and were ready to hop off the next morning.

From Clark Crichton Jr. (who many years later joined Huntley and me in the airline communications business) I got the full story of their trip down the coast. Dorbandt had been following the beach and had run into heavy snow a little east of Kolyuchin

BOY, 16, THRILLED BY SEA AND AIR TRIP FROM ARCTIC

Clarke Crichton and Five Others From Fur Trader Nanuk Will Have Happy Thanksgiving.

Home from a four-months' trip through the frozen seas between Alaska and Siberia, Clarke Crichton, 16-year-old Seattle schoolboy, was enjoying the greatest thrill of his life today, a reunion with his family in time for Thanksgiving.

Young Crichton, who has experienced more thrills this season than the average boy could in half a lifetime, arrived yesterday aboard the motorship Sierra from Nome to which place he went by airplane in successive stages from the ice-locked motorship Nanuk at North Cape, Siberia. The Nanuk was loaded with a million-dollar cargo of furs. Four hundred and fifty miles the youngster and five others, including his father, traveled over a sea of ice on a plane equipped with skiis until they settled down in the harbor of Nome.

Went North in June.

Crichton, with his father, shipped on the Swenson Fur Trading Company's motorship Nanuk June 15, bound for Bering Sea and Siberian ports on a fur trading expedition. Aboard the same ship were Olaf Swenson, head of the company; his daughter, Miss Marion, Broadway High School girl; Robert Gleason, University of Washington student and members of the crew. The father went as stewart and Young Crichton signed up as a cabin boy. He had never been to sea before and the long airplane ride he had across the Bering Sea was his first experience in the air.

The Nanuk is still ice-bound at North Cape and Mr. Swenson and Miss Marion are aboard, awaiting airplanes to carry them and the cargo of furs to Nome.

Transport Operations Delayed.

Transport operations in connections with those on the Nanuk have been delayed by a possible mishap to Carl Ben Eielson, one of the pilots who flew with Frank Dorbandt on the first trip out. When they started a return trip Dorbandt was forced down by bad weather at Teller while Eielson and his mechanic, Earl Borland, continued on. They reached the Siberian Coast and are believed now to be down at a point approximately sixty miles from the Nanuk. Alaska Airway officials, aided by natives, are conducting a search for the aviators.

ADVENTURES OF NANUK IN MAUL OF NORTH TOLD

Six Members of Crew Reach Seattle; Captain and Daughter Are Still Aboard Ice-Bound Ship.

From the bleak Siberian Arctic, where they were marooned for many weeks in the grinding ice floes, six men arrived in Seattle today with an interesting story of hardship and adventure. They sailed from Seattle June 16 for trading stations far to the westward from Bering Strait.

Caught in the maul of the Arctic, their little vessel is a prisoner at North Cape, where she will remain until the Arctic sun of next summer releases her fetters.

The six men from the Nanuk arrived on the motorship Sierra of the Arctic Transport Company from Nome. They were taken off the vessel in an airplane and landed in Nome. They are O. Holmstrom, M. Foley, G. V. Johansen, Clarke Crichton, Sr., Clarke Crichton, Jr., and George Hunter.

Also aboard the Sierra were Mr. and Mrs. A. Unden of Teller, and Ira Rank, fur trader of Nome and Seward Peninsula.

The Sierra brought reindeer meat, hides and $150,000 worth of furs.

Olaf Swenson, head of the Swenson Fur Trading Company, owner of the Nanuk, and his daughter, Miss Marion Swenson, former Broadway High School student, are still aboard the Nanuk, but will be taken to Nome by airplane in the near future.

Bay. After fighting it a while, he spotted a Chukchi village and landed near it on smooth sea ice.

Fortunately, Eielson, following a few minutes later, saw the Stinson, circled, and landed also. The Natives had heard them and quickly located the planes on the ice. They led all the travelers to their huts and took good care of young Crichton and the others for three days. On the fourth day the weather finally cleared and both planes were heated up, with Eielson and Borland helping Dorbandt get off first. About midway over Bering Strait, Eielson caught up with and passed the Stinson.

These flights proved that the pilots could land, wait for good weather—for days if necessary—and continue on successfully.

But the weather really began to turn ugly. Though both planes and crews were ready at Teller, the weather continued bad with snow and fog at North Cape. After four days of waiting, our weather was passable and it was good at Teller, so on November 9 both pilots decided to try it. Dorbandt soon returned to Teller reporting heavy fog over Bering Strait. Neither he nor his mechanic, Clark Bassett, had seen Eielson, who took off only ten minutes after they did. The Hamilton did not reach the *Nanuk* nor return to Teller.

Dorbandt reported trouble with his plane and did not take off again. Days went by, including at last a few days of wonderfully clear weather, but still Eielson and Borland did not show up anywhere.

THE SEARCH

HUTCHINSON COLLECTION

chapter 10

BY MID-NOVEMBER, EVERYONE WAS QUITE worried, and we knew from the press reports I copied daily from San Francisco and San Diego that the rest of the world was also becoming worried about the disappearance of the famed Carl Ben Eielson. Still, we knew the veteran flyer and his young copilot-mechanic had proved many times that they could land and take off in the North, and we hoped their difficulty was temporary.

November 18 was just another day until 3 p.m., when two

natives from Cape Serdtse-Kamen' arrived at the *Nanuk*. Swenson told me to ask Teller to stand by, he had some news. On the 9th, the day Eielson took off, Natives had gathered at one of their houses 60 miles from us. They saw Eielson come over just as it was getting dark; visibility was poor. Eielson circled the house twice but did not land. A Russian trapper 50 miles from North Cape heard the plane go over him, but he could not see it. He reported that it sounded as though the plane took a course inland toward the hills.

The natives who came to the *Nanuk* said visibility down their way had been good the past few days, which made it seem certain that Eielson and Borland must be in trouble. Swenson figured on sending a couple of dog teams there at once, and Dorbandt was again urging his headquarters at Fairbanks to send planes.

We were hoping that Eielson's failure to appear was due to some minor trouble such as too much snow for wheels, poor field, or even damaged landing gear, but the possibility that they might have crashed in the hills or hit rough ice in the dark was becoming stronger.

The Natives' report, of course, added to the concern about Eielson, and the pleas for search planes intensified.

Carl Ben Eielson was very well known in Alaska for his promotion of aviation, and especially for his efforts in obtaining the first contract from the Post Office Department to fly the winter mail routes. In 1924 he personally flew the mail from Fairbanks to McGrath, making all stops, and in a few hours accomplishing delivery that normally took 20 days by dog team.

These flights led to his employment by Hubert Wilkins, the Australian who was pursuing exploration of the still unknown Arctic areas by airplane. In the spring of 1926, Eielson returned to Fairbanks with the large Wilkins expedition which was to use Fairbanks and Point Barrow as bases for extensive Arctic flights. Unfortunately, both of their aircraft were damaged in test flights at Fairbanks, and Wilkins and Eielson were able to make only one short flight over the Arctic Ocean that summer. But Wilkins persisted in the face of ridicule, and by a daring flight in 1927 Wilkins and Eielson wiped out the lingering possibility that there was land directly north of Alaska.

In 1928, Wilkins and Eielson made a flight that gave them international recognition and acclaim. In a brand-new advanced-design aircraft, the Lockheed Vega, they flew from Point Barrow to Spitsbergen, traversing thousands of miles of hitherto unexplored Arctic. This flight of 20 hours and 20 minutes is still acclaimed as one of the astounding feats of early aviation. Wilkins was knighted, and honors were showered on both men by the United States and 14 other nations.

Instead of resting on this accomplishment, Wilkins organized an exploratory flying expedition to the Antarctic, and again took Eielson with him. These flights from Deception Island were the first in the Antarctic and resulted in the first discoveries of land from the air.

Eielson, rather than continuing exploratory work with Wilkins, now chose a different course. He returned to his dream of aviation's really serving Alaska, and his certainty that eventually Alaska would become a hub for air routes not only between America and Asia but even between Europe and Asia. He convinced the Aviation Corporation, which owned American Airways (now American Airlines) to buy some of the pioneer air services in Fairbanks and start a new company, Alaskan Airways. This was done early in 1929; Eielson was named vice president and general manager.

When the need for flights to the *Nanuk* at North Cape materialized, Eielson decided to lead the work on the new company's first large important contract.

When Eielson disappeared there were only two means of communication on the Arctic coast of Siberia: Communication was by radio, either from the *Nanuk* via Alaska or from the *Stavropol* via Srednekolymsk, Siberia. The *Nanuk*-Alaska-U.S. route was far faster, even for messages going to Moscow.

My position as radio operator made me chief of intelligence— like a small town telephone operator who is also publisher-editor of the only newspaper. I sent and received every word from the *Nanuk*, whether business, personal, press, or what have you. I continued to copy press sent by the big coastal radio stations at San Francisco and San Diego, and I also monitored traffic from Alaskan stations to the States—and even Russian traffic, because Swenson was fluent in Russian and I learned to copy it. We did not violate any laws, but were sometimes able to help ourselves and others stranded at North Cape just by knowing what was going on. Although my transmitting time was limited by the shortage of gasoline, I had no trouble keeping the battery-powered receivers in operation.

The search for the missing flyers began in earnest. At daybreak two dog teams, with Berdieff driving our team, left to search the coast. The pilots in Alaska were organizing to come over and help. Our weather became clear but much colder, down to 30 and 40 below; there was snow and fog at Teller and Nome. We hoped that Eielson and Borland were camping out somewhere.

On the 23rd the *Litke* arrived in Providence Bay and the Russians promised the planes they had brought would be ready to assist in a few days. The *Litke* reported new ice was a foot thick in Providence Bay, also that the 16 Russians who had left the *Stavropol* November 1 had just arrived at the bay, after a quick trip.

Soon we had another report from an Eskimo traveling up the coast, and it raised our hopes. He told us that he saw smoke in the foothills about 36 miles southeast of us. Swenson felt it must be Eielson and Borland as there were no natives in that area. We also heard that the Hamilton had loaded a case of eggs and 50 pounds of bacon for us, so they would have food.

On the 28th, Dorbandt at last took off at Teller but soon returned saying that his engine was not turning up properly. Other planes from Fairbanks had not yet reached Teller.

One day the *Stavropol* people told us the Russian planes were en route and they kept fires burning on the land area long after dark. The sun had gone down behind the hills for the winter on November 20, and hours of twilight were decreasing rapidly day by day. There was no word from Berdieff or the other dog teams we had sent down the coast.

On the 30th we had disappointing news. First, the captain of the *Litke* decided he could not hold his ship at Providence Bay any longer and would be forced to leave with the planes, which were having engine trouble in the extreme cold. Next, Berdieff returned and told us he had found no trace of the Hamilton. He brought conflicting stories from natives and Russians down the coast, but we still thought the plane might be in the foothills because Berdieff had traversed only the beach and lagoons.

On the other hand, we learned that a pilot named Joe Crosson, flying an open-cockpit Waco biplane, had arrived in Teller and was ready to come as soon as the weather permitted.

Our hopes of quick action were not to be realized. Storm after storm moved into either North Cape or the Seward Peninsula in Alaska, or both. The temperature frequently dropped to 40 below or even lower, it snowed heavily, and even when it did not snow the gales blew the snow, packing it so hard that we scarcely left tracks when we walked ashore. We knew this was ruining our airfield and I spent many hours looking and measuring and marking (with oil drums) the smooth areas, reporting results to Teller. We found that directly in the lee of the Cape it was still smooth enough for landings. The central part of the bay, so smooth before, now was covered with *sastrugi* (waves of hard packed snow) two and three feet high. They were having similar difficulties on the bay ice at Teller.

Several times Crosson and others who had reached Teller attempted to cross Bering Strait only to be driven back by storms and dense fog. Everyone was discouraged. The only favorable news was that the *Litke* and her planes were remaining in Providence Bay, but we had no word on whether they were able to fly.

We knew from the press reports that excitement over the efforts to find Eielson and Borland was increasing, and that plans were being made to send larger, better aircraft for the search. We heard that two Fokker Super Universals were flying up from St. Louis by way of Winnipeg, and that Aviation Corporation, parent of Eielson's company, was dispatching three Fairchild 71's via steamship. The 71's were new monoplanes like the Hamilton, with the pilot inside the cabin and room for six passengers.

Alaskan Airways had placed Dorbandt in charge of the search effort at Teller. In addition to Crosson in his Waco, Matt Niemenen, Ed Young, Harold Gillam and a pilot named Cope had reached Teller but none of their planes were really suitable for flights to North Cape. Only Dorbandt's plane had a cabin enclosing the pilot to protect him from the fierce cold, but we had come to feel from Dorbandt's reports to the Associated Press that he was mainly a publicity hound and would never come back.

Alaska's Governor Parks asked for a naval vessel to bring the planes to Seward; they would be brought to Fairbanks by train.

We began to get excellent broadcast reception from Pacific Coast stations, from Tokyo and from London, over the top of the world. We had no radio broadcast receiver, nor any loudspeaker, but my two receivers (each with only three tubes) covered the broadcast frequencies, both U. S. and foreign. When reception was very good, I used a long cord on a Baldwin earphone headset and hung the headset just over a wash basin placed on the after cabin table. Gathered around this improvised reflection speaker and remaining absolutely quiet, several persons could hear the news and music fairly well. Sometimes we even got East Coast stations, particularly WTIC in Hartford which was running all-night high-power test broadcasts.

On December 16 Aviation Corporation relieved Dorbandt and sent Alfred Lomen to Teller from Nome to take charge. According to Anderson, the Teller operator, everyone concerned was elated; Lomen was one of the best known and most respected businessmen in the Territory of Alaska.

At this time, I had some equipment trouble. First the engine governor stuck and the resulting high voltage damaged my motor starter; then the transmitter transformer burnt out a winding. Fortunately, I had spares, both mine and the *Elisif*'s, so I was able to make repairs fairly quickly. The gas engine got balky, and sometimes even Bill Bissner could not get it started in time for my schedules. And the storage batteries were in such terrible shape we couldn't keep 6 out of the 16 cells charged enough for my transmitter tube filaments. But Chuck Huntley had saved us by removing and packing for me the *Elisif*'s 12-volt converter. I wired it in with a spare field rheostat to drop the voltage so I was no longer dependent on the batteries. Bill took the batteries out and threw them over the side, because their glass jars were in danger of cracking and he could not save them.

On December 19, with fair weather at both ends, four planes took off from Teller but they returned one by one, Crosson being the last in after trying for two hours to get through, over, or under fog and snow in Bering Strait. On this same day we were advised that the three Fairchilds, with Arctic-experienced Canadian pilots and mechanics, had reached Seattle and were being put aboard the U. S. Coast Guard cutter *Chelan* for the trip to Seward.

December 20 was clear, almost calm and only 17 below. Despite clouds and fog at Teller, Crosson in the Waco and Gillam in a Stearman (both open biplanes) took off at 9:30 a.m. our time. They did not come back to Teller. We burned oil in our barrel markers long after dark but they did not show up. We could only hope that they had landed their planes, both on skis, somewhere down the coast.

The next morning, the shortest day of the year, first light came about 10 a.m. to a sky overcast but with fair visibility, and we watched to the eastward, hoping to see or hear the two small planes.

The hours dragged by. At 1:45 p.m., just as full darkness

was near, we heard a plane's engine and saw the little biplane approaching in the dusk. There was only one.

The pilot landed nicely and pulled up to the *Nanuk* and said he was Harold Gillam. He and Crosson had landed near Kolyuchin Bay the previous afternoon, stayed in a native hut that night, warmed up and took off together early that morning. But they soon became separated in fog and Gillam did not know whether Crosson had gone on or returned. Gillam stated again and again that he was sure the veteran pilot Crosson was okay and would reach us soon.

As Gillam was preparing to begin a search for Eielson and Borland the next morning, Crosson arrived, tired and worried about his young friend Gillam and relieved to find him safe at North Cape. After they had lost each other in the fog, Crosson had gone back and spent a second night in the native hut.

Harold Gillam arrives at 1:45 p.m. on December 21. He had flown the open-cockpit, single-engined Stearman almost 500 miles from Teller to Kolyuchin Bay to North Cape.

Joe Crosson with his Waco biplane (NC180E)
at North Cape, December 22.

Gillam and Swenson flew down over the foothills southeast of us where the Eskimos had seen smoke almost a month before. They saw a deer-native camp (which no one had known was there), searched some more, and finally returned to the *Nanuk*.

That evening Crosson and Gillam gave us the full story of their flights to the ship. They were, of course, flying only in twilight on these shortest days of the year above the Arctic Circle. After getting across the open water of Bering Strait under the fog, and being forced to go up over it at East Cape, they felt fortunate to see the shore near Kolyuchin Bay in the near darkness. Joe led the way down, spotted some native huts on the beach, and chose a landing spot on the ice nearby. Harold landed right behind Joe; both planes were on skis. The Chukchi, as always, took them in.

The next day when they became separated in fog, Crosson thought Gillam had turned back, so he also did and found the hut again. Gillam had continued up the beach in poor visibility. He had one narrow escape when he actually flew into a low hill. Fortunately, it had very gentle, smooth slopes and he simply bounced into the air on his skis.

Joe Crosson was a young but experienced Alaskan bush flyer, having come to Fairbanks in 1926, made many pioneering flights in the interior of Alaska, and even a trip to Point Barrow in an old Hisso-powered Swallow biplane. The flight to Point Barrow led to Eielson's taking Crosson with him on the Wilkins Expedition to the Antarctic in 1928. In November and December of that year, he and Eielson made some of the first exploratory flights in the Antarctic. Then, when Eielson had become manager of Alaskan Airways, Crosson again joined him. So now here he was, flying a small open-cockpit biplane north of the Arctic Circle in the dead of winter, searching for his companion and boss.

Harold Gillam had only that summer learned to fly in Fairbanks, and he joined Alaskan Airways. Although he had little experience, the eager, able young pilot prevailed in his desire to use the little Stearman to accompany Crosson to North Cape.

The two pilots in the little biplanes began the search using some gasoline they had brought and some low grade gasoline that the *Stavropol* lent them. They could search only when the visibility in the twilight was good; only two flights were made before Christmas. Swenson and Miroshnishenko went with them to point out the terrain and the native huts, and to act as observers. There was no sign of the Hamilton nor of the two missing fliers.

SWENSON PARTY EAGERLY AWAITING FLYERS TO BEGIN EIELSON HUNT FROM NANUK

By MARION SWENSON.

Special to The Times.

ABOARD THE MOTORSHIP NANUK, North Cape, Siberia, Thursday, Jan. 2.—We are looking forward with keen interest to the arrival of the Aviation Corporation's Eielson rescue expedition. We understand the Canadians will be at Nome today or tomorrow and then come on to the Nanuk as soon as weather conditions will permit.

A great deal of conflicting information has been published lately. The Moscow dispatches have proved especially confusing. All information from this end originates at North Cape and is sent out by the Nanuk's radio operator, Robert Gleason, or by the Russian trading ship Stravropol, three miles from us.

There are no other wireless sending stations closer than Anadyr and Seredni Kolimsk. So far the only information at all definite in its character has come from natives, who report having seen the plane at various places November 9 along the coast east of Cape Vankarem, as it was bound for North Cape.

A trapper about seventy miles east of here reported seeing the plane circling his hut and then proceeding west-

(Continued on Page 7, Column 2.)

110

GROUP ON NANUK WAITS EAGERLY FOR EXPEDITION

Miss Swenson Reports Conflicting Advice Regarding Eielson Disappearance in Ice-Bound Arctic.

(Continued From Page One.)

ward along the coast. About sixty-three miles east of here a Russian trapper and some natives heard the plane but could not see it, owing to poor visibility. A strong northwest wind was blowing and it was snowing slightly.

A native who heard the plane at the latter place made a search flight with Harold Gillam. He said the Eielson plane, judging from sound alone, seemed to be looking for a landing place. The noise of the motor was very distinct, even disturbing the Russian's dog team It appeared to be directly over the entrance to a lagoon.

The roar of the motor continued for several minutes, then stopped, but instantly started again, this time louder than before, then gradually died out.

Hope Exists.

We are hopeful of learning more in a few days, when the Nanuk's dog teams return from reindeer camps in the vicinity these reports came from. The teams have been held up several days because there was no dog feed, but yesterday natives killed two seals in an open stretch of water seven miles off Cape North. That meant meat for the dogs, and the men and teams accordingly got away yesterday.

Joe Crosson and Harold Gillam have thoroughly covered the area between North Cape and the Omwan River by plane. But they could not reach the deer camps without the use of the dogs. Today Crosson was to search the lagoons and the foothills between the Omwan and Cape Vankarem.

We are anxiously awaiting the longer days. Three to five minutes' difference is noticeable now and yesterday the sun was visible at an altitude of 5,000 feet.

HUNT PILOTS HOPE TO SURMOUNT FOG TODAY

Delayed again by fog and cold weather the Aviation Corporation's Canadian flyers, now in Alaska on an Eielson rescue expedition, were hoping to get away from Fairbanks for Nome today. They first planned to fly Tuesday but the extreme cold and the dense fog held them to the ground. The same conditions prevailed yesterday.

With the arrival of the planes at Nome the search for Pilot Carl Ben Eielson and Mechanic Earl Borland, missing since November 9, will be resumed with greater hope of success than has been possible in the past, those in charge of rescue efforts believe.

The planes are built to give the pilots the utmost protection possible from the elements, are equipped with motors which will enable them to fly under adverse conditions and are large enough to carry the necessary supplies of gasoline to make the 500-mile flight from Teller, Alaska, to North Cape, Siberia, where the fur trading ship Nanuk is locked in the ice, and still have fuel left for extensive scouting operations. Eielson and Borland were flying to the Nanuk when they were lost.

Christmas brought a severe storm, and we spent it together. Bill Bissner, who had become chief cook after Crichton's departure, fixed us a big reindeer roast and fruit compote. Marion's presence cheered us all, and everyone liked our new companions, Crosson and Gillam. The only flaw was that the Nome radio station failed to show up to take our many Christmas messages. I finally gave them to Teller, who managed to relay them to Fairbanks via the Nulato station. Later we learned that the Nome station had burned to the ground on Christmas Eve.

The storms of course caused great difficulty for the pilots. Despite their tightly wrapping canvas covers around the engines and cockpits, snow blew into everything. When the cold was extreme, they could not fully warm up the uncowled engines on the ground, so after heating the oil and engines with plumbers' furnaces they simply started the engines and took off immediately. On December 30 Gillam had difficulty getting started. When he finally got off his engine failed, and he was forced to land aft of the *Nanuk* on severely snow-hummocked ice. Neither he nor Miroshnishenko were hurt, but both landing gear struts were broken, and one lower wing and the cabanes (the mastlike wing

Harold Gillam and his Stearman.

Engine failure on takeoff brought Harold Gillam and the
Stearman biplane to a rough landing on the ice, December 30,
1929. Neither Gillam nor his passenger, Demetri
Miroshnishenko, was hurt. Gillam, Joe Crosson
and Russian engineers worked on repairs, and the
airplane flew three weeks later.

supports used on early biplanes) were damaged. Gillam and Crosson began planning repairs.

While this was going on, the Fairchilds reached Fairbanks on a special train and were being assembled. We also learned that the Russian government was sending four planes from Moscow to join the two at Providence Bay. The Russians offered a 2,000 ruble reward for any person finding Eielson's plane.

On January 3 one of the Fairchilds, flown by Canadian pilot Swartman with mechanic McCauley, had engine failure on takeoff in the extreme cold at Fairbanks and was severely damaged when it came down in the woods near the airport. The men escaped injury but the plane was damaged beyond immediate repair. The weather continued to be poor at North Cape; only one flight had been made since Christmas. The Russians were helping to repair Gillam's Stearman.

Two days later, the third Fairchild having been assembled and tested, two Fairchilds, with Canadian T.M. "Pat" Reid and Alaskan Matt Niemenen piloting, took off from Fairbanks at 9 a.m. They passed over Nulato at 11:30 a.m. At 1:30 p.m., Niemenen returned to Nulato but Reid kept going in bad weather. He failed to arrive at Nome. Reid had his mechanic, Bill Hughes, with him, also welder and mechanic Jim Hutchinson of Fairbanks, who was coming to North Cape to repair Gillam's plane.

With storm following storm, no word of Reid, and even the dog team searchers having a terrible time in the storms, cold and darkness, we were becoming discouraged. Crosson, Gillam and the Russian engineers continued work on Gillam's plane, while trying to keep the Waco in shape against the battering these fragile fabric-covered planes suffered on the ice without shelter.

On January 12 we had news. Reid was safe at Unalakleet on Norton Sound. Trapped in a mountain pass west of Nulato, he had landed on a small mountain stream. A wing tip struck a rock on the bank and was severely damaged. But Reid was fortunate, because in addition to his mechanic he had Jim Hutchinson along, with the fabric, glue, dope and other material they were bringing to repair the wing of Gillam's plane. Hutchinson, Hughes and Reid managed to repair the wing while camping out in the plane for seven days. They then made a perilous takeoff down the narrow river valley and flew into Nome.

That same day a native reached us with a letter from the Russian trader at Cape Serdtse-Kamen'. The letter said they had

Pat Reid's Fairchild. The repair job on the right-hand wing tip was done on an earlier flight, when Reid, Bill Hughes and Jim Hutchinson made a forced landing on a mountain stream west of Nulato, Alaska. They fixed it themselves and flew the airplane out.

heard the Hamilton going west on November 9, but had also heard it returning to the east a few hours later. Now we did not know what to think. Perhaps Eielson had gone all the way back to Alaska.

Gillam's repairs were nearing completion. Crosson and Gillam planned to search the river that flows to the sea just east of North Cape, and then go on to land at Cape Serdtse-Kamen' and try to find out whether other natives heard the plane returning. If they had, both pilots would return to Alaska.

Gales and snow permitted Joe to make only two more short search flights around the river while awaiting completion of work on Gillam's plane. A severe storm at Teller and Nome stopped all flying. There was no word from the Russians either. The sun came back and touched the top of North Cape, and that was wonderful to see.

Gillam's plane was ready on the 20th, and we watched anxiously as he took off on his test flight. The repairs held. The two Fairchilds arrived in Teller with Pat Reid and Ed Young at the controls; the two pilots said that they were ready to come over as soon as the weather permitted.

Snow and wind continued from the 21st to the 26th—then we came up with a fine clear day. Crosson and Gillam were up early, getting ready to go to Serdtse-Kamen' to trace the rumors that Eielson's Hamilton had been heard headed east. They took off at 9:30.

I was out on skis just after noon when Marion called, "Here comes a plane!"

We thought they had struck fog down the coast and had been turned back. Marion ran, and I skied, over to the plane as Joe landed and taxied to the ship.

He said, "The search is over, we found the plane."

It took a minute for this to sink in. Joe pointed to the forward cockpit, to a piece of corrugated aluminum. It was part of the wrecked Hamilton.

Some of the Russians and the ship's crew came running up and Joe had to repeat his statement. Harold landed a few minutes later and we all went to the after cabin for a conference. The pilots were looking pretty peaked; a glass of vodka braced them up a bit. Then we got the story.

As the planes were going down the coast, Harold flew two or three miles inland and Joe four or five miles further in. Fifty minutes out, Joe sighted a peculiar shadow cast on the snow by the

The *Nanuk* is silhouetted against the moon.
The ship was icebound at North Cape for nine months,
October to July, and for two months (November 20 to
January 18) they had no sun.

low sun. On circling lower, Joe saw the left wing of the Hamilton sticking out of the snow at 45 degrees. Seeing Joe circling, Harold came over. Joe picked a fairly smooth place on the tundra and landed. The surface was rough but he waved for Harold to land.

The Hamilton was a complete wreck. Eielson and Borland must have been killed instantly. It evidently struck while turning or banking to the right, because the right wing and landing gear were demolished and the left wing stuck up in the air, crumpled by the impact. The left landing gear, including wheel and tire, was intact. The motor and the pilot's cockpit had been torn off, and the motor was sticking out of the snow a hundred feet away from the fuselage. The cabin, although damaged, was intact. The fuselage had broken just behind the cabin and the tail swung around alongside. The cabin door was not jammed. When Joe opened it a slab of bacon fell out, showing that nothing had been touched, by man or by animals.

The crash had occurred about 10 miles inland and 90 miles from the *Nanuk*.

Joe and Harold stayed at the wrecked plane an hour and 15 minutes and dug around a bit, but they did not like the job so they returned to the *Nanuk*. We notified Teller and took the heat off Young, Reid, Niemenen and all the others concerned with the search effort.

The next day Crosson and Gillam took off early and flew to the wrecked plane, taking Demetri Miroshnishenko, Williams (one of our two sailors) and two natives. Berdieff and Jimmy Crooks left for the wreck at 3 a.m. with their two dog teams.

Crosson and Gillam stayed at the plane about two hours, and although all were digging as fast as possible, nothing was found of the two men. They dug the motor out and found the propeller wrapped around it and couple of cylinders broken off. The throttle was bent over wide open, indicating that the plane had struck the ground at full speed; they were not landing. The altimeter read 1,000 feet, which may have had something to do with their crash. The point at which the plane crashed was only 40 or 50 feet above sea level; if they thought they were a thousand feet up, they flew right into it. The clock had stopped at 3:40 p.m. Teller time—2:40 our time, about dusk.

Returning, the pilots spotted the dog teams, more than half-way there. Joe landed on the lagoon and gave them further directions so they would not miss the plane.

Nanuk's Captain, R. H. Weeding, stands beside
Joe Crosson's Waco biplane with pieces of
Carl Ben Eielson's Hamilton.

The wreck of Carl Ben Eielson's Hamilton monoplane. The wreckage tells the would-be rescuers how the crash occurred; it indicates that Carl Ben Eielson and his companion Earl Borland, must have died instantly. The airplane had crashed in a right-hand bank with the altimeter reading 1,000 feet and the throttle wide open. The right wing and landing gear were demolished, the motor and pilot's cockpit torn off and thrown a hundred feet, the fuselage broken in two behind the cabin. The bodies of the two occupants were found hundreds of feet from the wreckage three weeks later.

The digging for the bodies of Eielson and Borland in the wind-packed snow was arduous. Note how little of the shovels is embedded in the hard snow.

iNTERNATiONAL COOPERATION & RESCUE

chapter 11

ALTHOUGH THE WRECKED PLANE HAD BEEN located, much remained to be done. The men must be found and their bodies returned to civilization, the two small biplanes must get back home, gas must be brought in, people must be taken out, and all the fur should be carried to market. (The market was falling rapidly; the depression had begun.) The Canadians and Americans at Teller and the Russians at Providence Bay would still try to reach North Cape and complete the job.

On January 28 the weather was excellent at both Teller and North Cape; at 9:40 a.m. Teller time, the two Fairchilds piloted by Alaskan Ed Young and Canadian Pat Reid took off for the *Nanuk*.

Meanwhile the two biplanes returned from the wreck. Joe brought Demetri back because he had other work to do. They had found the second wheel of the plane, as well as revolvers, mittens, a seat and many other parts, but had not found the men.

Shortly afterwards, before 2 p.m., we saw the Fairchilds approaching. Young landed first, then Reid. Young's plane was U. S. registered (NC153H), Reid's Canadian (CF-AJK).

With the two Fairchilds on hand, Swenson and Marion began in earnest to prepare to leave, and the rest of us wished we could go too. Eielson and Borland still had to be found, though.

On the afternoon of January 29, two Russian planes appeared without any notice of their coming. The two Junkers came in high and went out over the *Stavropol*. One plane turned and came in downwind at the southwest end of the bay. He landed about halfway from the shore and headed toward the stern of the *Nanuk* on heavily drifted hard-packed snow. The first hundred feet were fairly smooth, but then the plane began to hit the bumps, still going fast because the pilot had landed tail up. The plane bounced time and again, 10 and 15 feet in the air, clanking like a steam shovel. It hit an especially big hump and the right landing gear strut broke. The plane came down on the wing and stopped.

The other pilot circled once and dived at the field against the wind. He came in right by the bow of the ship, and we all started to run. He was no more than 15 feet above the four airplanes parked there, and we thought he was going to wipe them out with his wing, but he zoomed up, circled, and came in again. This time he hit the ice about three-quarters of the way down our marked field and was soon on rough snow. He stopped just before the sand spit, without breaking anything. The second airplane had spare shock absorber struts to replace the broken strut on the first airplane. (Neither the ski nor the wing was damaged.) They also had brought a G.P.U. policeman and a police dog, but no gas. These Junkers airplanes had cabins for passengers but open cockpits for the pilot and mechanic.

Six planes of three nations were here now. Ours was the farthest-north international airport.

A message came to Joe Crosson, placing him in charge of U. S. and Canadian search efforts. Then I began to know what a

Top—The Fairchilds arrive January 28 at North Cape;
Ed Young's NC153H stands alongside Pat Reid's
Canadian CF-AJK.

Bottom—The next day the Russian flyers land with
their Junkers monoplanes.

Mavriki Slepneov, a bold and sure-handed pilot. Many times Slepneov set his airplane down in hazardous places for the benefit of the recovery crews.

Slepneov's airplane stands at the site of Eielson's wrecked
Hamilton with a house of snow blocks built under the
wing. Slepneov had flown his airplane down to the
wreck as a shelter for the diggers.

An international company thrown together by harsh weather and bitter circumstances. From left: Mavriki Slepneov, pilot and chief of the Russian rescue expedition; Galishev, a Russian pilot; Joe Crosson; Marion Swenson; two Russian mechanics; Ed Young, an Alaskan pilot; Bill Hughes, a Canadian mechanic; and Harold Gillam, an Alaskan pilot.

Airplanes of three nations (Canada, United States and
U.S.S.R.) flock around the *Nanuk* at North Cape. From left:
two Russian Junkers 233's, the Canadian and U.S.
Fairchild 71's, and Joe Crosson's Waco. The airplanes and
their pilots wait for work to do and weather to do it.
The Junkers low-wing monoplanes represent advanced
aircraft design; the open-cockpit Waco biplane
is a primitive thing by comparison.

real leader Joe was. Quietly, calmly, and without direct orders, he kept pilots, mechanics, Americans, Canadians and Russians working together to complete the search. Even Swenson marveled at the natural ability of this young pilot. Everyone except Harold Gillam was older and more experienced in many ways than Joe, but he really led.

Joe took the Russian flight commander, Mavriki Slepneov, down to the Hamilton, and on their return they reported that nothing new had been found except another pilot seat, this one badly crushed. The Russian pilots came out to the *Nanuk*, and the aviators had a big conference. The Russians wanted to help in any way they could, but they also wanted to take the *Stavropol* passengers to Providence Bay as soon as possible. They then received orders from Moscow to remain at North Cape and expedite the completion of the search. Slepneov decided to risk flying one of his Junkers down to the wreck, and he successfully landed near the Hamilton. This plane was then used as home for those digging in the hard-packed snow to find the bodies.

On Slepneov's return with Crosson, he came on board the *Nanuk* to complete his official report on the accident for the U.S.S.R. Swenson, as always, interpreted. Each aviator was questioned as to the cause of the accident. The consensus seemed to be that, flying low in very bad visibility in near darkness, with everything white, and without adequate flight instruments, Eielson had flown into rising ground while circling looking for a place to land. His report completed, Slepneov expressed the Russian government's condolences, then invited all the aviators to visit their headquarters on the *Stavropol* for dinner. This invitation was promptly accepted, even though it involved the three-mile walk over rough ice from the beach to the steamer. Captain Milozorov, who was convalescing from his near-death with pneumonia, had the *Stavropol* turned inside out to provide a lavish dinner. All stayed aboard overnight.

The diggers in the snow at the wreck were reinforced with sailors from the *Stavropol*, and Crosson and Gillam made flights there almost every day the weather permitted.

The critical need now was aviation gasoline, and it was decided that Reid would fly back to Teller to bring in all the Fairchild would carry. Swenson decided that he and Marion would go also and take with them Captain Milozorov, who was still very weak and anxious to return to civilization for medical treatment.

MARION SWENSON AND PARTY READY TO LEAVE NANUK

Seattle High School Girl, Father and Captain Expected to Fly to Teller Today With Pilot Reid.

By Associated Press.

POINT BARROW, Alaska, Wednesday, Feb. 5. — After being marooned for months on the fur trading ship Nanuk at North Cape, Siberia, Miss Marion Swenson, Seattle high school girl, her father, Olaf Swenson, head of the fur trading company which owns the ship and Captain Milovzorov of the Nanuk, were to take off today, if weather permitted, for Teller, Alaska.

Miss Swenson radioed here that they were to attempt the flight in a Fairchild plane piloted by Capt. Pat Reid, a Canadian aviator sent north to engage in the search for Pilot Carl Ben Eielson and Mechanic Earl Borland, American aviators who were lost November 9 while plying from Teller to North Cape. The wreckage of the Eielson plane was found January 25 in a lagoon ninety miles southeast of North Cape, but the bodies of the aviators have not yet been located.

Return With Fuel.

Reid, Miss Swenson said, was to take on a heavy load of gasoline when he reached Teller and return to the Nanuk so that other planes at the ship would have fuel to continue their trips to the scene of the wreck. Miss Swenson has announced that on their arrival at Teller, she and her father would fly to Nome and Fairbanks from where they would travel by rail to Seward and then proceed to Seattle by steamship.

Joe Crosson, one of the pilots who found the wreck, accompanied Commander Slipneov of the Russian planes at North Cape to the wrecked Eielson plane, where the Russian flyer was to remain until the bodies

After several days' wait the weather appeared favorable, and on February 7 they took off, making the flight to Teller in just over four hours. Reid later took them to Nome. They were then flown to Fairbanks and proceeded by train to Seward and by steamer to Seattle, arriving there March 1, 1930. After seven months together, we on the *Nanuk* missed them very much.

Marion was a lovely young girl, strong and healthy, always cheerful and excited to be marooned in the Arctic as she had secretly wished. Swenson's only son had died at Nome from diphtheria in 1921, but Marion, the older of his two daughters, had all his desire for adventure in the Arctic.

Being the two youngest persons on the *Nanuk*, we were of course drawn together often and gradually became quite fond of each other. But a small ship, icebound with a crew and a very watchful father constantly in attendance, is not very conducive to romance. Perhaps it will suffice to say that the arrival of the aviators and Marion's departure saved the situation. But she did change my life markedly, and I remained an admirer of hers until she died. She was a brave, beautiful, young woman.

Marion Swenson and her father leave the *Nanuk*. The five persons on the flight are, from left: Bill Hughes (mechanic), Olaf Swenson, Captain T. M. "Pat" Reid (pilot), Marion Swenson and Captain Milozorov of the *Stavropol*. They are preparing to board Reid's Fairchild for the four-hour, 500-mile flight from North Cape to Teller, Alaska; the date is February 7, 1930. The Swensons' and Milozorov's journey continued by air to Nome and Fairbanks, thence by train to Seward and steamship to Seattle, where they arrived on March 1, 1930.

We still had Joe Crosson, Harold Gillam and Ed Young, and we spent many hours comfortably aboard the *Nanuk* while the wind howled in the rigging. Bill Bissner was the mainstay, doing most of the cooking, from pancakes in the morning to reindeer roasts and even fruit compote on our best days.

On the 10th of February and again on the 12th, Reid started out alone from Teller with a full load of gas for us, but both times he was forced by fog to turn back at Bering Strait. On the 16th he made it as far as Cape Serdtse-Kamen' and spent the night in a native hut. He cached his load of 200 gallons of gas there and returned to Teller.

Earl Borland's body was found on the 16th and Eielson's on the 18th. Both had died instantly in the impact of the crash, and their bodies were thrown hundreds of feet when the engine and most of the nose section were torn from the fuselage.

On the 21st, Reid started out alone again with full tanks and 200 gallons of gas in the cabin in five gallon cans. He had good weather except for some fog near Kolyuchin Bay, which he was able to surmount, and he was soon over the Amguema River and over the wreck. He saw Slepneov's Junkers and Gillam's Stearman and, mistaking smoke as a signal, decided to land. Landing close to the Junkers, Reid hit a sharp ridge of the wind-packed snow. A ski broke, and the plane slewed around and wiped off the landing gear entirely. The loss of the gear was fortunate, really, because it prevented a sudden stop and the load of gas behind Pat did not shift forward to crush him. He was not hurt at all, even though one ski crashed through the cabin, and the cans of gas were not broken. But he was chagrined over his second accident in the same Fairchild, again badly damaged far from assistance.

Gillam brought Reid to the *Nanuk*, and they began plans for salvage of the Fairchild. These would include bringing Jim Hutchinson, the master welder who had been with Reid in his first accident, all the way from Fairbanks with acetylene tanks, tools and material.

Meanwhile the Junkers was made ready, and the bodies of Eielson and Borland, which had been on the tundra for more than three months, were loaded aboard and flown by Slepneov to North Cape. They were taken to Demetri Miroshnishenko's building, where they were thawed out so they could be placed in sleeping position and allowed to refreeze. On the morning of March 4, the bodies were brought out by the Russians on flag-draped sleds and,

Slepneov arrives with the bodies after a 90-mile flight from the wreck of the Hamilton. The bodies are thawed in a heated building, placed in a sleeping position, and allowed to refreeze.

after some short speeches, delivered to the Americans and placed aboard Ed Young's Fairchild. *Nanuk*'s flags were at half mast.

It had been agreed and approved by the U.S. and U.S.S.R. that Slepneov in the Russian Junkers would accompany the bodies to Teller, Nome and Fairbanks. The valiant Harold Gillam went with them in his self-repaired Stearman. Crosson and Reid flew with Young in the Fairchild. The three airplanes made it to Teller without incident and reached Fairbanks on March 10, four months after Eielson and Borland were lost.

On the morning of March 4, the Russians bring out Carl Ben
Eielson's and Earl Borland's bodies on flag-draped sleds and
deliver them to the Americans.

Inset—Mavriki Slepneov is seen here at the brief transfer
ceremony. The pilot to his left is probably Galishev; the
names of the others are not known.

The bodies of Eielson and Borland are loaded aboard
Ed Young's Fairchild for the flight to Alaska.

THE LONG WAIT FOR ESCAPE

chapter 12

FOR THOSE OF US LEFT AT NORTH CAPE, THE finality of the tragedy set in and we felt a lonesomeness that was hard to shrug off. Crosson's Waco was still alongside the ship, and Reid's Fairchild lay on her belly near the wrecked Hamilton.

In a few weeks Joe Crosson came back with a new Alaskan Airways pilot, S. E. Robbins, each flying Fairchild 71's. They brought mechanic Herb Larison who was to go down to the wreck and begin the repair of Reid's plane. Hutchinson was to be brought over later to do the welding. Gasoline, tools and repair materials constituted the balance of the load, except coffee, cigarettes, mail and a few personal items for us.

After weeks of work and several flights to Teller, as well as many trips from North Cape to the wreck in the Waco and by dog team, Hutchinson and Larison had the Canadian Fairchild ready. Hutch and Herb had dug out a cave in the snow under the plane, which greatly facilitated the welding and the attachment of the landing gear struts, axles, skis and fittings. When all was ready, they dug a ramp for the skis to the top of the snow, and Joe Crosson taxied up the slope to the surface. Taxi tests proved the repairs were excellent and Joe took off to the *Nanuk*, where Hutchinson and Larison completed their work.

Then, with Crosson's faithful Waco NC180E overhauled, gassed and ready, the last aircraft departed May 10 (Crosson flying CF-AJK and Robbins in NC180E) and all aviation activity at North Cape ceased. The excitement was over.

On the *Nanuk* we settled into a spring routine. The captain and I washed off the soot in the after cabin as best we could, and I moved into what had been Marion's room. Berdieff moved into the room left by the mate, and the two sailors occupied our old room. All our extra bunks had been in use while the aviators were with us.

Bill Bissner continued to do most of the cooking, and the sailors and I rotated KP duty. The captain overrode his stated democratic intentions and refused to wipe a single dish.

It was during this period that the greatest sorrow of my trip occurred. I received messages of condolence and then the news of my father's sudden death.

Berdieff, now a good dog handler, made two trips to the *Elisif* and brought back gasoline for my engine. The captain would not let me go anywhere overnight for fear I'd miss taking some message. I started to repair the winch motor armature and salvaged enough of the coils to operate it on 180 volts instead of 220.

I had started a daily exercise plan when there was no flight activity, and I now carried this out every day regardless of the weather. My exercise included hikes to the top of North Cape and some push-ups. Bill kept busy, and we went hunting regularly for seal, and later for ducks and geese.

The sailors defied the captain and began bringing Native women aboard. One seaman, Hearn, was completely insubordinate and the skipper would have put him in the brig if he had one.

Top—Pat Reid's Fairchild lies on its belly in the snow with the skis and landing gear wiped off and the propeller bent.

Bottom—The airplane has had its landing gear replaced by Jim Hutchinson and Herb Larison, but still it needs a new propeller.

Top from left—Sailors Williams and Hearn, Jimmy Crooks,
Captain Weeding and Chief Engineer Bill Bissner
loaf on the afterdeck of the *Nanuk*. Crooks spent the winter
on the *Elisif* salvaging cargo. The other four (and the
author) wintered on the *Nanuk*.

Bottom—The salvaged winch motor armature, which the
author rewound to run on 180 volts instead of 220.

The author, *Nanuk*'s radio operator and
assistant engineer, Robert J. Gleason.

Gleason's mentor, the chief engineer, William P. Bissner.

The captain daily drank the vodka the Russians gave him for all of us, and he slept most of the time. He never left the ship, never helping with hauling ice for water, and never hunted. May and June were long months aboard the *Nanuk*. I stuck with Bill Bissner.

With continuous daylight and the warmth of June, our cabin fever began to thaw. Now that the position was vacant, I signed on as assistant engineer, which raised my pay from $115 to $225 per month. Bill and I began to overhaul the big diesel engine. We took the dog house off the companionway, cleaned up the ship, got out the sails, reinstalled my repaired winch motor and got ready to get out of there.

During the latter part of June, the ice around the ship became rotten, and we had to be careful when hunting or going ashore. Finally, a little earlier than the previous year's July 29th break-up, the *Nanuk* and the *Stavropol* were freed. On the morning of July 8, 1930, a light southerly wind and gentle currents allowed even the *Stavropol* to escape without danger. I spent the morning on top of North Cape taking pictures of the breakup.

The *Stavropol* came around the cape, blew her whistle at us, and started down the coast. Captain Weeding decided to wait a bit, but the next day, after good reports from the *Stavropol*, we headed south.

Swenson had bought another ship, the Danish motorship *Karise*, to replace the *Elisif*, and he was en route toward North Cape as he had been in the *Nanuk* the previous year. We arranged to meet the *Karise* near Cape Vankarem. We were glad to see Swenson but happier still to be on the way out. Swenson brought Captain Carl M. Hansen, of Amundsen's northeast passage fame, to be first mate on the *Nanuk*. Bill and I worked around the clock in the engine room; I was doing my radio operating on the side.

The trip down the coast was nothing like our trip north the previous summer. The Chukchi Sea was wide open. We anchored off Nome briefly on July 17, took on a little diesel oil and headed for Dutch Harbor, which we reached on the 22nd. If only we had had two weeks of open water like that in September, 1929!

From Dutch Harbor to Seattle we had a most remarkable trip. Almost all the way it was not only calm, but flat—the North Pacific had no swells at all. I'm told this may not happen in a lifetime. With all sails up, but idle, we chugged along for 10 days, reaching Cape Flattery August 1 and docking in Seattle at 11 p.m. August 2, 1930.

Top—The ice begins to melt at North Cape in mid-June.

Center—By late June, the snow covering the sea ice has begun to melt.

Bottom—Free! Breakup comes and *Nanuk* is released, July 8, 1930.

NANUK FREED FROM ICE; TO JOURNEY HERE

Famous Eielson Quest Ship Released From Long Imprisonment Off Siberia.

By Associated Press.

MOTORSHIP NANUK, North Cape, Siberia, Tuesday, July 8.—The icy embrace of the Arctic Ocean has at last released its grip upon the American fur trading ship Nanuk and the Soviet steamer Stavropol, held icebound here since last September.

The Nanuk was freed late Sunday when the packed ice moved offshore, while a little later the ice broke up in the bay freeing the Stavropol. The Russian ship, which was frozen in three miles offshore, worked in through a lead during the night to an anchorage alongside the Nanuk.

The crews of both ships are prepared to depart for their respective ports as soon as conditions warrant, the Nanuk for Seattle and the Stavropol for Vladivostok, Siberia.

It was the Nanuk that American aviators, Carl Ben Eielson and Earl Borland, were flying from Teller, Alaska, last November when their plane crashed near North Cape, killing both of them.

Ice-Freed Nanuk Sails For Seattle

NOME, Alaska, July 17.—(A. P.) —The American fur trading ship Nanuk arrived at Nome today from North Cape, Siberia, and sailed a few hours later for Seattle, her home port. The Nanuk was frozen in off North Cape last September and was only recently released from the grip of the Arctic ice.

Nanuk on Way Here

DUTCH HARBOR, Alaska, Tuesday, July 22.—The power schooner Nanuk, under command of Captain Weeding, was continuing her voyage to Seattle today after a stop here for oil and water.

The ship was bound to Seattle after being ice-locked in the Siberian Arctic for several months. It was while flying to the Nanuk with provisions that Carl Ben Eielson and his copilot, Earl Borland, lost their lives last fall.

Nanuk lies at Dutch Harbor on her passage home. She stops only briefly, at Nome July 7 and at Dutch Harbor July 22 for oil and water, and then she heads south.

151

When *Nanuk* docked at Seattle, the headline
proclaimed, END OF AN ARCTIC SAGA.

SEATTLE POST-INTELLIGENCER

The familiar Puget Sound ferryboat is a hometown sight.
Nanuk docks at Seattle's Bell Street Terminal
at eleven o'clock on a Saturday night, August 2, 1930.
She and what remains of her crew have been away
for 13 months and 18 days.

From almost every standpoint, the voyage had been a disaster. Less than half the fur had been taken out; two lives had been lost; one airplane had been destroyed and three other airplanes damaged. The *Elisif* was lost. Despite all this, I felt as though I had participated in a pure and heroic adventure. The dedication, perseverance and tenacity of crew and pilots, and the ability of men without adequate equipment and facilities to cope with cold, wind, darkness and adversity, made this a tremendous experience, which I did not—and never will—forget.

Epilogue: *Nanuk*

Two years after this voyage to the Siberian Arctic, *Nanuk* was chartered by Metro-Goldwyn-Mayer for use in the feature film "Eskimo: Mala the Magnificent." Loaded with movie people and equipment, she was taken to Teller, Alaska, in the summer of 1932 under the command of Captain Carl M. Hansen and deliberately frozen-in there. On board were a complete talking-picture crew, with a famous director (William S. Van Dyke), a famous author (Peter Freuchen, who wrote the book on which the screenplay was based; he also played the role of the captain of the *Nanuk*) and Anna May Wong, who portrayed the Eskimo heroine. An Eskimo supporting cast spoke in their own tongue, and their words were translated by subtitles on the screen. The film editor won an Academy Award, but the picture was a box-office failure. MGM added some hot Hollywood igloo scenes and reissued it, and it was still a failure.

MGM purchased the *Nanuk* in 1933 and made her into the *Hispaniola* for "Treasure Island." Later she became the *Pandora* for the first American filming of "Mutiny on the Bounty."

In 1941, the Maritime Research Society of San Diego reported that she was "laid up at Long Beach." Nothing has been heard of her since; she has probably been destroyed.

Similar vessels, the schooners *Wawona* and *C. A. Thayer,* which were built in the same period by Hans Bendixsen, builder of the *Nanuk*, may be seen at maritime museums near Seattle and in San Francisco. Although they are larger than the *Nanuk*, their hull models, fir timbers, construction, rigging, cabins and fittings are the same.

Appendix:
The Men, the Ships and the Airplanes

AIRMEN

Earl Borland, mechanic for Carl Ben Eielson.

Calvin Cripe, mechanic for Noel Wien.

Joe Crosson, Alaskan Airways pilot; flew Waco biplane NC180E and Fairchild 71's.

Frank Dorbandt, Alaskan Airways pilot; flew Stinson Detroiter.

Carl Ben Eielson, Alaskan Airways pilot and manager; flew Hamilton monoplane.

Galishev, Russian pilot; flew Junkers 233's.

Harold Gillam, Alaskan Airways pilot; flew Stearman biplane.

Bill Hughes, Canadian mechanic for Pat Reid.

Jim Hutchinson, Alaskan Airways master welder mechanic from Fairbanks.

Krashinsky, Russian airman.

Herb Larison, Alaskan Airways mechanic.

Leongard, Russian airman.

Alfred Lomen, Nome, who was hired by Aviation Corporation to direct the search for Eielson from Alaska.

McCauley, Canadian mechanic for pilot Swartman.

Matt Niemenen, Alaskan Airways pilot.

Captain T. M. "Pat" Reid, Canadian pilot; flew Fairchild 71 monoplane CF-AJK.

S. E. Robbins, Alaskan Airways pilot; flew Fairchild 71's and Waco.

Mavriki Slepneov, Russian flight commander; flew Junkers 233's.

Swartman, Canadian pilot. Valvitca, Russian airman.

Noel Wien, Alaskan pilot.

Ed Young, Alaskan Airways pilot; flew Fairchild 71 NC153H.

AIRPLANES

Fairchild 71 enclosed-cabin, high-wing monoplanes, with 425-hp Pratt & Whitney Wasp engines. U.S. registry NC153H flown by Ed Young and Joe Crosson. Canadian registry CF-AJK flown principally by Captain T. M. "Pat" Reid, later by Joe Crosson.

Hamilton "All Metal" cabin monoplane with 425-hp Pratt & Whitney Wasp engine. U.S. registry NC10002, flown by Carl Ben Eielson (and, in the winter of 1928-1929, by Noel Wien).

Junkers 233 enclosed-cabin, open-cockpit, low-wing monoplanes, with 300-hp liquid-cooled engines. German-built. Flown by Mavriki Slepneov and Galishev.

Stearman open-cockpit biplane, with 220-hp Wright Whirlwind J5 engine. Flown by Harold Gillam.

Stinson Detroiter. Four-passenger cabin biplane with 220-hp Wright Whirlwind J4B engine. Flown by Frank Dorbandt.

Swallow biplane with Hisso aircraft engine.

Waco open-cockpit biplane, with 220-hp Wright Whirlwind J5 engine. U.S. registry NC180E, flown by Joe Crosson.

RADIO STATIONS AND OPERATORS

U.S. Army Signal Corps radio stations in Alaska: Fairbanks, Nome, Nulato, Point Barrow, Teller.

U.S. Navy radio station at Saint Paul Island.

J. H. Anderson, Signal Corps station at Teller.

Baburin, Russian steamship *Stavropol*.

Jack Dowd, Signal Corps station at Nome.

Joe Drummond, Signal Corps station at Nome.

Robert J. Gleason, schooner *Nanuk*.

Charles "Chuck" Huntley, motorship *Elisif*.

Charles "Chuck" Huntley, motorship *Elisif*.

RUSSIANS

On steamship *Stavropol:* Baburin, radio operator. George Kretschman, expedition meteorologist. Milozorov, captain.

Pilots: Galishev. Mavriki Slepneov, flight commander. Both flew Junkers 233's.

Demetri Miroshnishenko, government agent at North Cape.

SAILORS AND FUR TRADERS

Jimmy Crooks, worked for Swenson on Siberian coast.
Captain Jochimsen, ice pilot on *Elisif*.
Even Larsen, captain of *Elisif*; from Brevik, Norway.
Ray Pollister, business associate of Olaf Swenson.

On *Nanuk*:
Tzaret Berdieff, Russian-born U.S. citizen, interpreter for Swenson party; supercargo of *Nanuk*.
Bill Bissner, chief engineer.
Clarke Crichton, cook and steward.
Clarke Crichton Jr., 15, cabin boy.
Arnold Draven, second mate.
M. "Paddy" Foley, seaman.
Captain Carl M. Hansen, first mate on voyage home.
James "Hearn" Hearn.
O. Holmstrom, first mate on outbound voyage.
George Hunter, assistant engineer.
G. V. "Vic" Johansen, seaman.
Marion Swenson, 17, daughter of ship's owner.
Olaf Swenson, proprietor of Swenson Fur Trading Company and owner of ships *Elisif, Karise* and *Nanuk*.
R. H. Weeding, captain.
"Willie" Williams, seaman.

The Crichtons, Foley, Holmstrom, Hunter, Johansen, Marion Swenson and her father, Olaf Swenson, were flown out in November, 1929.

SHIPS

Chelan, U.S. Coast Guard cutter.
Dupont, launch used to deliver explosives to *Nanuk* at departure from Puget Sound.
Elisif, motor schooner owned by Olaf Swenson.
Haida, U.S. Coast Guard cutter.
Karise, Danish motorship purchased by Olaf Swenson in spring of 1930.
Kolyma, Russian steamship.
Litke, Russian icebreaker.
Nanuk (formerly *Ottilie Fjord*), motor schooner owned by Olaf Swenson.
Northland, U.S. Coast Guard cutter.
Ottilie Fjord, former name of *Nanuk*.
Sierra, motorship of Arctic Transportation Company.
Stavropol, Russian steamship.
Victoria, steamship of Alaska Steamship Company, Seattle.
Wisconsin, steamship of States Steamship Company, Portland, Oregon.

Bibliography

Beaglehole, J. C. *The Life of Captain James Cook*. Stanford: Stanford University Press, 1974.

Cook, James. *Voyages of Discovery of Captain James Cook*. London: Ward, Lock, Bowden & Co., 1882.

Crichton, Clarke, Jr. *Frozen In*. New York: G.P. Putnam's Sons, 1930.

Daws, Gavan. *Shoal of Time: A History of the Hawaiian Islands*. New York: Macmillan Co., 1968.

DeLong, Emma. *Voyage of the Jeannette*. Boston: Houghton Mifflin and Co., 1883.

Grierson, John. *Challenge to the Poles*. Hamden, CT: Shoestring Press, Inc./Archon Books, 1964.

Kennedy, Kay J. *The Wien Brothers Story*. Booklet (38 pp., 5½" x 8½") published by Wien Air Alaska for the Alaska Centennial Purchase Year, 1967.

Lyman, John. "Pacific Coast-Built Sailers 1850-1905." *The Marine Digest* Installment No. 26, (July 26, 1941) Maritime Research Society of San Diego.

Mirsky, Jeannette. *To the North*. New York: Viking Press, 1934.

Newell, Gordon. *The H. W. McCurdy Marine History of the Pacific Northwest.* Seattle: Superior Publishing Co., 1966.

Newspapers, 1929-1930:
Fairbanks Daily News-Miner
New York Times
Seattle Times
Seattle Post-Intelligencer.

Nordenskiöld (Nordenskjöld), Nils Adolf Erik. *The Voyage of the Vega Round Asia and Europe.* New York: Macmillan Co., 1881.

Potter, Jean. *The Flying North.* New York: Macmillan Co., 1947.

Ray, Dorothy Jean. *The Eskimos of Bering Strait 1650-1898.* Seattle: University of Washington Press, 1975.

Reid, T. M. (Pat). "The Search for Carl Ben Eielson." *Canadian Aviation Historical Society Journal,* 1968.

Smith, William D. *Northwest Passage.* New York: McGraw-Hill American Heritage Press, 1970.

Stefansson, Vilhjalmur. *The Adventure of Wrangell Island.* London: Jonathan Cape Ltd., 1926.

Swenson, Olaf. *Northwest of the World.* New York: Dodd, Mead & Co., 1944.

Wien, Noel. "First Round Trip Flight—North America to Asia." *Wien Alaska Arctic Liner,* Fall 1961.

Wilkins, George H. *Flying the Arctic.* Knickerbocker Press, 1928.